Sunken Garden Poetry

1992–2011

With support from Hill-Stead Museum
& the Connecticut Humanities Council

sunken garden poetry
1992–2011

Brad Davis, Editor

WESLEYAN UNIVERSITY PRESS

MIDDLETOWN, CONNECTICUT

Wesleyan University Press

Middletown CT 06459

www.wesleyan.edu/wespress

© 2012 by Hill-Stead Museum

All rights reserved

Manufactured in the United States of America

Wesleyan University Press is a member of the Green
Press Initiative. The paper used in this book meets
their minimum requirement for recycled paper.

Library of Congress Cataloging-in-Publication Data

Sunken Garden poetry, 1992–2011 / Brad Davis, editor.

   p. cm. — (Garnet books)

Includes bibliographical references and index.

ISBN 978-0-8195-7290-5 (cloth : alk. paper) —

ISBN 978-0-8195-7291-2 (pbk. : alk. paper) —

ISBN 978-0-8195-7292-9 (ebook)

1. American poetry—Connecticut. 2. American
poetry—21st century. I. Davis, Brad, 1952–
II. Sunken Garden Poetry Festival.

PS548.C8S86   2012

811'.540809746—dc23   2012001476

5 4 3 2 1

Photograph on pages ii and iii courtesy of Morrow Jones.

Photograph detail on page v courtesy of Cynthia Cagenello.

Contents

Foreword

Out of the union of two distinct elements—poetry and garden—grew a marvelous child. Full of wonder and promise in her infancy, this prodigy dazzled us all with her poise and sense of self, the hoards of admirers she attracted, the magic and beauty that effortlessly descended in her presence each summer evening. Over the years, this child grew in grace, animated by the generous impulse to bestow some order and understanding on her small corner of the world. This twentieth anniversary anthology represents her coming of age, and we at Hill-Stead Museum believe the volume conveys a true sense of the distinct nature of our summer-long poetry festival—accessible, intimate, often unpredictable, and warmly human.

Though a landmark, this book is not a history or a legacy. It's an invitation to join an audience, perhaps even to visit Hill-Stead some week during the summer to experience a remarkable poetry phenomenon that is alive and thriving. In the spirit of Theodate Pope Riddle, Hill-Stead's visionary humanitarian and architect who opened her home to art and literature and the community, we invite you to wander down the maple-lined drive with hazy vistas of the Connecticut hills before you—old stone walls on either side—pass by the wondrous big white house and descend into the Sunken Garden to revel in the poetry on these pages and all that is yet to come.

Mimi Madden
Artistic Director, Sunken Garden Poetry Festival

Sue Sturtevant
Director, Hill-Stead Museum

Sunken Garden circa 1902. *Photograph by Gertrude Kasabier, courtesy of the Hill-Stead Museum*

Editor's Acknowledgments

Thanks are due to the many who helped assemble this book. First, to the community of sixteen assisting editors, Connecticut poets all, each of whom read through the festival's archived set lists from one of the nineteen seasons and selected the poems for that year: Lonnie Black (1992), Rennie McQuilkin (1993), Ravi Shankar (1994), Steve Foley (1995), Robert Cording (1996), Kate Rushin (1997), Pit Pinegar (1998), Ginny Connors (1999), Gray Jacobik (2000), Pat Hale (2001), Sue Ellen Thompson (2003), Steve Straight (2004), Margaret Gibson (2005), Wally Swist (2006), Jim Finnegan (2009), and Norah Pollard (2010). And sharing thanks with these sixteen, two more assisting editors: Amy Russo for selecting representative poems from the set lists of our college student readers (2008–2011), the winners of the Connecticut Poetry Circuit contest; and Mimi Madden for selecting from contest chapbooks (2000–2011) the representative poems from our Connecticut high school readers, the winners of Hill-Stead Museum's "Fresh Voices" competition.

Second, heartfelt thanks to the staff of Hill-Stead Museum who believed in and supported the project from the moment it was proposed, especially Sue Sturtevant (Museum Director and CEO) whose vision for poetry's integral place in the life and outreach of the museum has reanimated all things Sunken Garden and made this book possible; as well to Mimi Madden (Artistic Director, Sunken Garden Poetry Festival), Amy Russo and Sarah Wadsworth (Poetry Festival Coordinators); and to those who helped cobble together the one hundred-plus festival readers' set lists from old audio tapes, videos, and DVDs: festival interns Kristin Bergman, Gabrielle Campagnano, Suchi Mandavilli, and Chelsea Pepe; and volunteers Billie Alban, Karen Althammer, Katharine Carle, Carol Fein, Morrow Jones, Shirley Keezing, Jim Kelleher, Peter Madden, Rennie McQuilkin, and Bernita and Ralph Sundquist.

And here is it also appropriate to extend Hill-Stead's thanks to the many who helped birth and nurture the festival that this project celebrates: editor Lary Bloom and the staff of *Northeast* magazine, including staff editors Anne Farrow and Steve Courtney, and designers Patricia Cousins and Joe Hilliman; sound designer David Budries (Chair, Sound Department, Yale School of Drama) and the various technicians who created audio archives and recorded programming for National Public Radio; broadcast professionals Phyllis Joffe, Nancy Cobb, and Bessy Reyna who worked with Budries to produce interviews

Courtesy of James Rosenthal

with festival poets and festival samples heard Saturday mornings for several summers on NPR's *Morning Edition*; and finally Sarah McQuilkin and Cindy Smith, whose flower arrangements have graced the Sunken Garden stage from the beginning.

Third, much gratitude to Wesleyan University Press, the staff of which not only surprised us at the museum with their instant enthusiasm for the idea of the book but were patient and gracious with me, a newcomer to the ins and outs of editing such a volume. In particular, we are most grateful to Suzanna Tamminen (Director and Editor-in-Chief), Parker Smathers (Acquisitions Editor), Leslie Starr (Assistant Director and Marketing Manager), and Patrick Cline (Intern).

Finally, highest thanks to the scores of poets who have read at the Sunken Garden Poetry Festival—the pros, up-and-comers, and students—and to the extraordinary audiences who braved all manner of seasonal weather to make this twenty-year-old, summer-long festival the institution it has become and on whom the festival's future success is wholly dependent. This is a book by a community, of a community, for a community—past, present, and future—and it has been my honor and great pleasure to serve as its editor.

September 2011

Introduction

For two decades, the Sunken Garden Poetry Festival has attracted poets and audiences — *large* audiences — to the extraordinary, high-walled, one-acre garden of Hill-Stead Museum in Farmington, Connecticut, to "taste and see" the Whitmanesque magic of poetry (and music, too) in the open air. This book ushers you back through twenty seasons in that word-charged garden.

As the featured poets line up in these pages for their metaphoric return to the festival microphone, one poem per festival appearance, we recommend stepping outside for as long as you plan to read, preferably late afternoon, the sun about to set. But before you lose yourself in the poetry, two of the festival's prime movers, Lary Bloom and Rennie McQuilkin, share a bit of how it all came to be.

🌿

In the summer of 1986, prodded by poet Lonnie Black, I tried an experiment in *Northeast*, the *Hartford Courant's* weekend magazine — announcing a "poetry party" to occur just three evenings later, with readings by Black, Sue Ellen Thompson, and Rennie McQuilkin. The Joseloff Gallery at the University of Hartford would hold, we estimated, about 125 people — plenty of room for the few dozen we expected. But by thirty minutes before show time, it was clear it would not be large enough. More than 300 people showed up, and, as the evening progressed, those who couldn't get in stood outside the Gallery's French doors, holding umbrellas in the rain, straining to hear the words of the poets inside.

The following year, we moved the party to Trinity College, and again it drew a large crowd. So when, in February of 1992, on a bitter-cold day, Rennie Mc-Quilkin came to *Northeast* with Sarah Lytle, Hill-Stead Museum's director at the time, to propose a summer poetry festival and ask for *Northeast's* backing, they instantly got the answer they sought. Here we had Hill-Stead, long famous for its architecture and priceless Impressionist paintings, willing to put itself on the line financially, and to make full use of its gorgeous sunken garden. Here also was Rennie, a well-recognized poet with a big vision for the benefits of public readings by American masters.

I'll let Rennie say more about those early years, except to add that, sitting Wednesday evening after Wednesday evening in that beautiful garden I heard among audience members laughter, sighs of recognition, and, yes, sobs. What they heard in the well-chosen words of festival poets had great relevance to

From *left to right*, Lonnie Black, Rennie McQuilkin, and Lary Bloom. *Courtesy of Pit Pinegar*

their own lives. There was also, early on, outrage. During the first season, at the utterance of the first four-letter word in the garden (words that weren't spelled l-o-v-e or r-o-s-e) two women snapped up their lawn chairs and stormed out. But, complaints were few and enthusiasm great. As I wrote in *Northeast* on the tenth anniversary of the festival: "In a poetry reading, all manner of subjects are put forward. It isn't as if real life is avoided. Quite the opposite—poets touch on matters too truthful to talk about in pleasant company. And yet the Sunken Garden seems to be something of an escape, too. Those walls protect us from any mischievous northeast winds, from the memorandums of the corporate world, and from the pummeling of ordinary headlines."

What we helped start in a magical spot in Farmington, Connecticut, has continued and flourished because of the work of those who followed us, who built on an idea born on a steamy summer night at the Joseloff Gallery more than a quarter of a century ago.

I have often felt sorry for people who haven't been to our festival, who haven't availed themselves of a festival evening's change of pace and the society of poets who seem to have better answers for us than our therapists. We happy few (not so few, in fact) have found a way to make those summer evenings slow down, and even, in important ways, last forever.

Lary Bloom

When the festival opened in June of 1992, some 800 poetry lovers descended on Hill-Stead Museum to hear Hugh Ogden read his work, creating the first of many "poetry traffic jams," as noted by the *New York Times*. The evening's enormous success was augmented by a bass viol player, invited by Hugh to precede and accompany his performance, and by Emily Holcombe, who read responsively a section of Hugh's poem "Lecture on the Tides." I can still see Emily's light shining out in the darkened audience as she repeated the lines "Even you who are lost will always / be here as long as the moon / circles into its line with the sun / and the oceans respond."

Even on the icy day in February of 1992, when Hill-Stead Director and festival co-founder Sarah Lytle took me into the Sunken Garden to assess it as a venue for poetry, its high stone walls and *Secret Garden* atmosphere suggested that it could become what Galway Kinnell later called it: "this little paradise for poetry." (It is pleasant to realize that the root meaning of *paradise* is *sunken garden*, as Mark Doty pointed out during his reading in the summer of 2011.) The Sunken Garden is truly a paradise when it is in full bloom, responding to the loving care with which Hill-Stead volunteers have restored it to its original nature conjured by Beatrix Farrand in 1920. The Festival has delighted and edified hundreds of thousands over the years, demystifying poetry, making it a living, breathing presence, a performance art as well as a literary one.

Poets around the country and beyond have come to see the Sunken Garden as one of the finest poetry venues anywhere. In the words of Stanley Kunitz, twice the country's Poet Laureate: "Poetry is somewhat different when it's read in an open space instead of a closed auditorium; this brings it closer to its origins in early choral dance. The Sunken Garden is one of the very best settings for a poetry reading in the whole country. A beautiful open space, a sense of a flowering world, and also a very responsive and large audience." Pit Pinegar, herself a festival poet and director of the festival's Hartford Student Poetry Outreach, describes the experience of sitting in the Sunken Garden thus: "There is something about sitting in the garden in a lawn chair tilted back a little, at dusk, listening to a generation's best — James Merrill, Stanley Kunitz, Richard Wilbur come immediately to mind — listening to the words, being absorbed by them, feeling almost a physical part of the language — and utterly present; and then looking up to see a jet from Bradley International Airport, at 7,000 feet or so, creep slowly across the sky. It is as though I can hold in my hand the best of what life has to offer." And this from Bessy Reyna, who has twice delighted us with her readings in the garden: "There are times when, in the middle of a snowstorm, I think about a lovely summer night when I am sitting in the Sunken Garden listening to poetry, surrounded by hundreds of people. That thought helps me, a woman from the tropics, to be able to endure yet another winter in Connecticut. Because the Sunken Garden Poetry Festival is not only about poetry—it is about friendship and love, it is about our willingness to publicly share our emotions with others as we listen to words that touch us or make us laugh."

As Kunitz observed, audiences at festival events are exceptionally responsive. There is none of the biblical silence that sometimes deadens indoor readings. In the outdoor atmosphere of the Sunken Garden, applause comes spontaneously and vigorously, and so do sighs and laughter. Perhaps audiences are inspired not only by the joy that comes from hearing superb poetry read superbly, but by the beauty of the garden with the sun setting behind the stately elm on Hill-Stead's front lawn or the moon rising over the shoulder of the evening's poet; by the songs of the resident mockingbird that always seems to take its cues from the music of poetry; by lambs bleating in the nearby pasture while low-flying bats design the sky. Anne Farrow describes the opening night of the 1993 season thus: "It was a June evening of complete beauty. I remember that the air was full of the most extraordinary and powdery golden light. I felt like I was in a Merchant Ivory movie, encased in the golden atmosphere. Those wonderful hills to the north were illuminated like a painting, and I knew that I was absolutely blessed." There is magic in the separate peace we enter in Hill-Stead's *secret garden*. Where else would children and adults alike break into dance during musical preludes and where else would a poet's young son (Martín Espada's Clemente) run up to the podium and announce, "This poem's about me!"

But a garden always has its serpent. In the case of the festival, that serpent was the fire-breathing sky. During the first season, rain seemed to fall almost every poetry night. Still, we were hardy and moved into Hill-Stead's Makeshift Theater, which made shift to house many more of us than might have pleased the fire marshal. I remember one stormy night with particular pleasure. Sue Ellen Thompson was at the podium, reading a poem about her parents dancing in the kitchen like newlyweds. No sooner had she pronounced the memorable line, "I never saw my father naked," than a bolt of lightning struck just outside the Makeshift Theater with a deafening clap. The podium light flickered and sparked, and there was a moment of terrible silence before both audience and poet broke into guffaws of laughter. Dave Perbeck, the museum's long-time Head of Security, rushed to shut the slatted sliding door behind Sue

Ellen, and the reading went on, not without our renewed faith in the gods' sense of humor.

Rain was so often an issue that Garret Condon, a frequent contributor of *Northeast* poetry articles, referred to approaching Wednesday evening storms as "Poetry Fronts." But one summer the rain spared us miraculously on several occasions. There was hail in Glastonbury, trees were blown down in Bristol, lightning strikes crippled West Hartford, but Farmington was Camelot. Calls came in from worried audience members all over Hartford County, and we said simply, "Come on over. It never rains on Hill-Stead." Perhaps that was too tempting. I believe it was the evening of June 21, 1995, just before Cheryl Savageau's reading, an evening when the weatherman reported a zero percent chance of rain, when a black cloud formed directly over Hill-Stead. For about half an hour it poured. Then the sun came out, we wiped off the chairs, the sound equipment emerged unscathed, and the show went on.

And it was a good show, just one of more than a hundred we have enjoyed over the years — shows featuring many of the country's finest poets. More than a few of them have been past or future U.S. Poets Laureate: Stanley Kunitz, Robert Pinsky, Billy Collins, Maxine Kumin, Richard Wilbur, Robert Haas, Donald Hall, and Philip Levine. Others have been recipients of major national awards: Sharon Olds, Marge Piercy, Carolyn Forché, and Sonia Sanchez, to name just a few. A number gave their first major reading in the garden and went on to greater glory, such as Natasha Trethewey, who recently received the Pulitzer Prize in Poetry.

It's not just my recollections of the "major poets" that I relish. In fact, the phrase "major poet" is inappropriate, since less well-known poets have provided some of the most memorable moments of all. I recall with special joy Norah Pollard's two remarkable readings, the second of them at the end of the 2006 season. I'd like to think that one reason the festival resumed after the hiatus year of 2007 is that so many of us remembered the remarkable beauty of Norah's reading under the stars. Her father Red Pollard rode Seabiscuit again during that reading, Jim the Van man revived a drowned fly by pouring salt over it, and the poet's brother dared a speeding locomotive to cowcatch him, then at the last second rolled down a bank to the blessed safety that comes of risking everything.

Such scenes depicting life's better side have been etched in our memories by two decades of Sunken Garden poets. I wish there were time to mention all their startling performances. We carry in our hearts their joys and sorrows, their passion and honesty, and their beautiful voices, each so distinct and resonant that when we read their work on the page, we still hear them on stage. There are not words for the many gifts they have given us.

Music was, from the start, an integral and essential part of the experience of the Sunken Garden. It has sometimes been folded into performances, as when Kent Hewitt and Tim Moran performed during Margaret Gibson's memorable presentation in 1998, and when Gwyneth Walker fiddled her original musical versions of Lucille Clifton's poetry, with lyrics sung by Denny Walker. On the latter occasion, a fruitful rivalry between musician and poet developed. The beauty of Gwyneth's musical interpretations so impressed the poet that she was energized and sent forth her words to vie with their musical counterparts. Because of Gwyneth's music, Lucille's performance was, she later told me, the best of her illustrious career. Many other poets have been inspired by festival music, such as Hayden Carruth, who in 1998 was so impressed by the performance of the Hugh Blumenfeld Trio that he changed his whole reading, choosing a number of poems based on his early days as a drummer in a Chicago jazz group.

Other musical features have included a klezmer band from Congregation Beth Shalom in Chester, Connecticut (with Lary Bloom himself on keyboard), and saxophonist Paul Winter. I will never forget the amazement and joy felt by everyone in the garden when, thanks to the magic of sound engineer David Budries, wolves accompanied Paul Winter, seeming to bay from distant corners of Hill-Stead's several-hundred acres. The international music group Sirius Coyote provided other memorable moments. Anne Farrow has written of the group's performance in 1997, just a few days after the tragic death of John F. Kennedy, Jr. and his wife in a plane crash off Martha's Vineyard: "At one point a tall musician stood all by himself and blew on a conch shell. It made a low, rushing sound, like moving water. Very slowly he turned to each corner of the immense crowd, and blew once on the shell. All you could hear was its falling echo, and the wind making its silvery rattle in the trees."

As the 1990s moved toward the Millennium, the word was out. More and more people began showing up on Wednesday poetry nights. Over 2,000 arrived in 1999 for an Irish Night featuring Irish step dancers, Irish music, and the celebrated Irish poet Eamon Grennon, then teaching at Vassar College. On that occasion, the evening's event occurred on the Great Lawn in front of Hill-Stead, as it did for Lucille Clifton's appearance. The festival was threatening to outgrow the garden. Still, we found ways of fitting into it on all future occasions, finding lovely new nooks and crannies. Happily, David Budries, the Festival's enormously gifted sound engineer, has from the very beginning been able to create a rare 360-degree sound system, allowing audience members to lie back, close their eyes, and drink in the music of the Muse, even if their view of the performers has sometimes been less than perfect.

Every festival aficionado and performer will have his or her own stories of interesting moments in the garden. Elizabeth Kincaid-Ehlers recently spoke of the thrill she felt when looking out at a darkened sea of faces while a full moon added to her podium light, shining on the poem she was reading. The first time I read in the garden, when I came to a poem about carrying my recently departed father's belongings in my arms, a skyful of stars brought him so close to me that I had to catch my breath and fight back tears. I don't believe such a moment would have occurred at an indoor reading. *Poetry under the stars*, to use Lary Bloom's phrase, is a rare experience for everyone involved. During Marilyn Nelson's first reading in 1992, she was reading "Star-Fix," in which her father, a Tuskegee airman and the navigator in a Flying Fortress, is guiding the bomber back to base after a dangerous mission, "shooting the stars" with an octant. As Marilyn's words evoked that moment in the life of her long-dead father, we all heard the deep drone of a large, prop-driven, no doubt military aircraft in the distance. It may have been a transport on its way to Bradley International, but we knew better.

When you come to the garden, be ready for such moments. The most recent one I can remember occurred during Mark Doty's season-ending reading in 2011. As Mark's energetic voice electrified the audience, some thing or one just beyond the Garden's western wall began to make a sound, which I took at first to be an attempt to imitate the inimitable voice of the poet. But when the sound took flight and sailed across the sky behind Mark, Polly Brody (who knows her birds) leaned forward from the row of chairs behind me and said, "Did you see that Jay?" I'd known the Jay is an excellent mimic and often imitates the *kree* of a hawk, but I'd never known a Jay could mimic Doty.

Ancillary events have also been an important part of the Sunken Garden Poetry Festival, such as the marvelous seminars on alternate Wednesdays, led by Steve Straight. (He himself gave an inspired reading in the garden, a reading that started my granddaughter on her career as a poet.) In his role as seminar leader, Steve put everyone at ease, facilitated lively discussions of the previous Wednesday's poet, and had his seminarians play "poetry games" which often led to some excellent writing.

In 1993, Dan Doyle of the Young Writers Institute at Kingswood-Oxford School suggested that a Night of Fresh Voices featuring high-school poets be added to the festival. At first, I was skeptical, but as a teacher I knew that young people can rise to an occasion in ways that their elders scarcely believe. My leap

Courtesy of James O'Gorman

of faith was rewarded beyond my wildest expectations! Each year since then, the winners of Hill-Stead's high school competition have given stirring and startling performances. I say *startling*, since one never knows what those Fresh Voices may voice. Anne Farrow has noted that the young poets have issued "some of the frankest language ever heard in the Garden. The student readings have an unfettered quality." And, I might add, an absolutely delightful one!

Fresh Voices has grown steadily since it was inaugurated and, eleven years ago, spawned the Hartford Student Poetry Outreach. Under the leadership of Pit Pinegar, poets as celebrated as Bessy Reyna, Elizabeth Thomas, Ernie Blue, Kate Rushin, and Pit herself have gone out into Hartford high schools to provide year-long workshops, generating an interest and literacy in poetry that has led to much excellent writing and also a whole new group of festival audience members. It is wonderful to see so many young faces in the Sunken Garden.

A logical sequel to the Fresh Voices Competition was the Sunken Garden Poetry Competition for adult poets inaugurated by my able successor Alison Meyers and expanded by Cindy Cormier during her fruitful years as Artistic Director. Most recently, the current Artistic Director, Mimi Madden, and Hill-Stead Director, Sue Sturtevant, have done a great deal to make the festival a year-long series of programs featuring frequent workshops, readings, and other events, not to mention a Hill-Stead Book Club and a literary journal, *Theodate*,

Courtesy of Cynthia Cagenello

whose editor is the poet/teacher Brad Davis. The vision of Hill-Stead Museum as Connecticut's premier center for poetry led to the first annual Hill-Stead Poetry Party in April 2011, an event at which all state poetry groups were given a chance to expound upon their activities. The large number of poets who attended this event is further testimony to the fact that Hill-Stead and not just its Sunken Garden has become a *paradise for poetry*.

There is much more that may be said about the Sunken Garden Poetry Festival, but in the end what matters most is that the festival has become one of the world's largest and most successful endeavors of its kind, one that has made poetry a living, breathing art form for thousands from Connecticut and beyond, and one that tells us the American public is hungry for the sort of artistic and literary riches offered by poetry and its musical analogs. Long live Hill-Stead as a *little paradise for poetry*.

Rennie McQuilkin
August, 2011

1992

*I looked and saw a long line of cars snaking up
to the mansion. It was like a scene out of* Field of Dreams.
—*Sue Ellen Thompson*

Poems selected by Lonnie Black

Featuring

Hugh Ogden

Sue Ellen Thompson

Charles Darling

Marilyn Nelson

Pit Menousek Pinegar

Pam Nomura

Emily Holcombe

Steve Foley

Elizabeth Kincaid-Ehlers

David Holdt

Susan Gimignani Lukas

Rennie McQuilkin

Fingers

Because a trooper was down on all fours
at night hunting your finger tips,

because cars were lined up side by side
and a six wheeler besides, lights on to help,

because cruisers arrived and just plain
ordinary cops who got down and looked,

because the great belt of highway was
closed and the hearts of so many drivers

opened to a teen-age girl and the search
for lost parts, because the trooper

found your forefinger and cried
and someone else your middle finger,

the one that touches everything first,
and then your ring finger, now

more precious than any jewel,
because ice that turns lips blue kept

your fingertips cold while
the lights flashed red and the sirens,

because a nurse put her hand on your
brow and whispered and someone

sewed and another prayed and all
that had been severed was linked:

praise and praise again
the fingers and hands that sifted

the gravel-glass-rubble by the roadside
seeking the lost ones, praise the woman

who held your other hand on the long
ride to the hospital and kept talking,

praise the intern who first lifted
your fingers from the tray and placed them

at the end of your hand and the surgeon
who threaded a needle and joined

nerve to nerve and wound the tendons
under the quiet light of the operating room,

praise the nurse who washed your face
and lay your bandaged hand beside you

and sat with you as you came up
out of anesthesia into recovery,

and praise to you, your terror and rising
again so that someday a girl might become

a woman who will touch a man's breast
and feel his heart beating the way

her own heart beat that night, a mother
who will caress the hair of her child

and say to her when things are lost,
how all was lost and found again

because strangers got down on all fours
and picked up pieces of my body.

Remembering My Parents' Sex Life

They danced in the kitchen
while supper was on —

bodies pressed, Glen Miller,
all six burners on the old Caloric

flicking their skirts of flame,
the tuneless buzz

of my father's hummed accompaniment
like an insect trapped

beneath the music —
pure interlude, six children

in ten years. A pinch,
a slap, flesh resonating

its applause,
a dip and sweep

among the tapping pot-lids,
scattered cats and chairs.

They showered late at night —
disappeared and reappeared

in full nocturnal dress.
No bleating springs,

no sharp intake of breath
and never anything

above the flannel sheets
but one head breathing sleep

into the other's nape.
I never saw my father

naked and am grateful now
for that, grateful

that I came into my knowledge
innocent and late,

that someone had to teach me
everything except the music

which I danced to,
when my time came,

as if born to it
in all that steam and clatter.

CHARLES DARLING

In Certain Lights

I

On the day-trip to Linesville, my son
pretends to sleep in the back seat, tries
to ignore my father, up front with me,
who names every church and cemetery we pass,
the people he's married and buried in each.
If my father's mind were a garden,
every morning something new would grow and still
he would know the name of every vegetable.
In this dream-garden, my mother stands among

the sharp utensils of harvest, ready to commit
their summer's labor to the variegated jars
lining the basement walls with liquid light.

II

Why has my father brought us here?
The carp at Pymatuning have little in common
with ordinary fish like the knife-edged trout
that carve through water. Bloated,
with vacuum-cleaner mouths, they swallow
at once whole loaves of day-old bread the tourists
toss from the walkways. On Tuesdays
the truck from the cat food factory comes down
to haul away its nameless mess of fish.
My father has seen this before
so it doesn't surprise him: miracle of fish in air,
violence of water and light in the awful nets.

III

The next day, over P.S. 34, innumerable dark birds
are practicing end-sweeps they someday
will use to take over the city. Often,
on summer evenings, my mother watches
their rising up and settling back,
their troubled exercises over the church
where my father has preached for thirty years.
Swift or swallow? Too small for starlings?
My father would know. My mother, who doesn't hear
the question, only sweeps her arm across the glass
as if she were tossing to the birds
a handful of nothing but grace notes.

IV

On the time zone's western edge, the days
last longer than they do out east.
After their mutual 80th birthday dinner,

in what light is left, I pose my parents
for a picture outside the lakeside restaurant
beside a mock-orange bush. My father points
toward the darkening blossoms which seem
about to bend to touch my mother's hair.
He smiles as if he were a guide, as if this thing,
by virtue of his having known its name,
has been suddenly, inexplicably improved.

V

There are walls in my parents' apartment
where whole families can live forever, politically
symmetrical in their similar black-trimmed frames.
Looking at the picture of my father holding me
like a tiny Buddha, I am as amazed
at my father's white shoes as I am
at my mother's height. Also the plethora
of uncles, so many I'd forgotten their names:
Donald, Francis (the one that just escaped
the Tennessee at Pearl), Jimmy, Heinrich . . . , Heinrich?
Below: me in overalls, skinny and big-eared,
no glasses; my grandmother's gimp-legged dog.

VI

Naomi, my parents' dog, is dying. She piddles
anywhere, unpredictably and hopelessly, and my father
pursues her from room to room with handfuls
of pink paper towels. After my son and I leave tomorrow,
my father will gather her up
in his arms and carry her down to the vet's
and submit his clear, incontrovertible instructions.
Too early to ask will there be a replacement
to accompany an old man on his long walks
to the cemetery. Squirrel-chaser, flower-uprooter,
who shall hear my father's sermons now?

Before we leave, my son and I pose
before the dark open mouth of the garage.
I notice it's hard to smile and hold in my stomach
at the same time. I notice my mother's hands,
like crazed porcelain, holding the camera.
What I want, I suddenly realize,
as I pack within easy reach the oatmeal cookies
and the soft lemon squares dusted with sugar,
is for my parents to live forever, like gods,
like trees in a wood so dense they can't fall down.
Driving away, we wave to my mother waving,
my father already turned to his garden.

MARILYN NELSON

Star-Fix

for Melvin M. Nelson, Captain USAF (ret.) (1917–1966)

At his cramped desk
under the astrodome,
the navigator looks
thousands of light-years
everywhere but down.
He gets a celestial fix,
measuring head winds;
checking the log;
plotting wind-speed,
altitude, drift
in a circle of protractors,
slide-rules, and pencils.

He charts in his Howgozit
the points of no alternate

and of no return.
He keeps his eyes on the compass,
the two altimeters, the map.
He thinks, *Do we have enough fuel?*
What if my radio fails?

He's the only Negro in the crew.
The only black flier on the whole base,
for that matter. Not that it does:
this crew is a team.
Bob and Al, Les, Smitty, Nelson.

Smitty, who said once
after a poker game,
I love you, Nelson.
I never thought I could love
a colored man.
When we get out of this man's Air Force,
if you ever come down to Tuscaloosa,
look me up and come to dinner.
You can come in the front door, too;
hell, you can stay overnight!
Of course, as soon as you leave,
I'll have to burn down my house.
Because if I don't
my neighbors will.

The navigator knows where he is
because he knows where he's been
and where he's going.
At night, since he can't fly
by dead-reckoning,
he calculates his position
by shooting a star.

The octant tells him
the angle of a fixed star
over the artificial horizon.

His position in that angle
is absolute and true:
Where the hell are we, Nelson?
Alioth, in the Big Dipper.
Regulus. Antares, in Scorpio.

He plots their lines
of position on the chart,
gets his radio bearing,
corrects for lost time.

Bob, Al, Les, and Smitty
are counting on their navigator.
If he sleeps,
they all sleep.

If he fails,
they fall.

The navigator keeps watch
over the night and the instruments,
going hungry for five or six hours
to give his flight-lunch
to his two little girls.

PIT MENOUSEK PINEGAR

Shamaal

Arabic for "wind from the north"

I walk. My daughter rides
her bike, stopping to pick
flowers and stones, bringing
back her treasures against
a wind so strong she puts

her shoulder to it like
a lineman into a dummy
at spring practice. She
picks a spray of lantana
and hands it to me. A blossom
snaps off and rolls —
faster than I can walk,
faster than I can run —
pink and yellow kaleidoscoping
to a speck of coral,
lost in the distance.
Rounding a bend, I head
north into the gale,
wind and sand reducing
my eyes to slits in yellow
air. The lantana hurtles
south across the desert,
perhaps caught, finally,
on acacia thornes. Wind-
blown, I step into my walled
back yard, but it is no quieter
there: a whirlwind
traps dried bougainvillea
petals in a frenzied flowering —
rasping like the songs
of wraiths — and spins them
in a blood-red vortex.

PAM NOMURA

The Golden Thread

In the YMCA locker room,
I stand naked before the mirror,
mesmerized by dark blue veins

streaked across my breasts that are
so full of milk they ache.

In the sauna's insatiable heat, I am dry
timber; old growth that sizzles alive
with every drop of sweat or milk that drips
down my body, and I cannot take my eyes
off the veins, running like rivers over my skin.

And I cannot stop wishing that I had held you then,
that first summer you were a ranger and I was so
afraid of each rung on your fire tower ladder
until I cleared the trees and the Lolo Range took shape below.

After weeks of being alone, you were quiet.
And when we talked, you spoke to me with your back turned,
scrutinizing the valleys, squinting into the last slice of sun
as it charged the river below with fire. "It does that

every sunset," you said, "a golden thread through the forest."
Only then, did you speak of your mother
and cancer, and home. When you
finally turned to me, I did not hold you, or even
take your hands, while you told me you were lost.
"What will I do?" you said. "She was my golden thread,
the one I followed through the maze."

Over your shoulder I watched thunderheads
scud across distant ridge tops, lightning slash,
and in its wake, flames tear into the darkness
like signal-fires racing from Troy to Greece.

Who do they burn for tonight? I wanted to ask.
But you were busy at your station; calling your number
into the radio, citing landmarks, charting graphs.

Not knowing what else to do, I went out on the platform
to watch the rolling smoke and flame. But you, your duty done,

looked only down-mountain for the unalterable blue
of the Bitterroot flowing at the foot of the range, a blue
so etched in your heart, you could run all its branches
on a night with no moon.

EMILY HOLCOMBE

Praying in Marquand Chapel after Cancer Surgery

Fourth of July.
Sky's popping on its skin
      with green dandelions
      red tendril vines
      blue glories of morning light
      framed on night, and
      white, bright arcs
that take the heart outside itself.

Inside here,
it's muffled:

in here, it's mostly dark and I barely
find the first pew. I sit:
Lord, it's right by you.
The table, the wine, the bread; and in my mind I see instead
the table where they led me and said,
"Please get on"; and I did,
head on hard metal.

I remember tonight the hands laid upon me:
the nurse's hands, which wrapped me warm
      and strapped me firm.
the technician's hands, which linked my chest
      to the machine that mapped my heartbeat.
the anesthetist's hands, which fed sugar and sleep into my veins . . .

and the surgeon's hand — the hand that fended off pain:
 at the instant the needle plunged into the back of one hand,
 his eyes saw and
 his fingers, poised, pressed down on my other arm.

 No pain, no memory of pain,
 only this:

Lord, answer me —
if it is love that sanctifies,
is that why I knew, when their eyes looked down on me,
and I stared up,
it was not the operating room, not the operating table,
that is the sanctuary,
but it is I, it is they, seen by You:
 cancered and cut,
 sewing and sewn,
 body and blood,
 in the skin and fire of the night?

STEVE FOLEY

Angel

sings in my classroom
until I tell her no
Christmas carols,
TV jingles,
the latest from Madonna,
each note light like a piccolo played cleanly
on a hill above a stream,
and when I pass out books to read Shakespeare aloud
she commandeers the star part
and makes Juliet sing
a Capulet cantata of whole note prithees,
quarter note wherefores,

banishèds in scat,
and with the signal of the bell
Angel whistles out the doorway,
hums her locker combination,
gives voice to the hallway on her path to the bus
that will haul her out of town,
past stockaded yards full of in-ground pools,
tiled patios, flowers,
haul her on the highway
headed to the city,
as far as her block,
where some buildings have windows,
some windows have glass,
where some stairwells have no one
fast asleep on them, where some apartment doors
aren't identified in chalk,
where some living rooms have heat,
where some fathers live at home,
where Angel, undoubtedly,
sings well into the night.

ELIZABETH KINCAID-EHLERS

My Mother's Closet

My mother's closet sloped.
Shoes mated in odd positions.
Boxes stacking the back wall
kept the eaves from plummeting
to the hard, narrow-boarded floor.
Afternoons, I drifted through the quiet
from one closet to another. Hers
was best, I could smell her there.
Stroking rayon, satin, silk, I nosed
around perfumed breasts of blouses
to collars where, on tiptoe, I could tuck

my head and dream. Turning my face away
from falsely scented seams,
I wrapped long sleeves around me.
Or, more rarely, I might squat
to try those troubling odors
in the places where her lap would be.
Oh, it was risky. I had been forbidden.
Getting caught was certain
and the consequence secure: pain, long
silence, then the ridicule. But I was a fool
for love, so I returned to kneel among
the tumbled buckles, straps and heels.
Shamed by deprivation, wondering
at my own dumb need, I pulled the surplice
of her skirts about me and sought some place
beyond. Detached from sadness, blame or anger,
I breathed my way back to my mother
until, in that imagined, motionless dark,
we were at one.

DAVID HOLDT

Deer Crossing

For years I've taught that William Stafford poem
in which he finds a doe, dead on the road.
Her fawn, unborn, alive and doomed, is sacrificed
as if it were a poem he could not write.
Last Winter on the Avon Mountain road
I hit a deer. I stopped and stood beside
the woods and toed the dust, accused
by all the lights lined up behind.
Two wooly men, beer labels on their baseball caps,
dropped from their van to offer help.
Their heavy boots joined in my dance.

They were both hunters; they knew the ropes.
They told me I could keep the deer.

A wild-eyed woman stepped up then,
demanded that I "do something." I
scuffed more sand. Turn, turn again.
I said "My baby daughter's in the car."
I said "I'll turn myself in to the law."
She said "Oh sure!" Assigned to me
the guilt for some crime resonating
in her head. She stalked away
as if to say that this was not the way things end.

In the arc-lights of the station-house lot
the Avon cop confirmed the deer was mine.
He said someone had turned me in;
had told them I would never stop or call,
could tell that in the red glow of the lights
that blinked in counterpoint to darkness
on that hill. Well she was wrong.
I saw that angry woman one more time.
She was talking to the statue of the stag
in Bushnell Park, as if he were the champion she required.

This spring a student from my class
stopped in to say a deer had hit his truck; had hit it
like a snowball out of season. It almost seemed
the deer were striking back, an organized guerilla war
on those still innocent enough to travel through the dark.
My young friend took his deer home in the truck.
To butcher the damned thing took half the night.
This poem means to tell him you did right;
you need not carry guilt, it only makes more
crazy people in the parks. I checked it, Fred,
that statue's bolted to the ground. It lacks
the breathing wilderness that haunts our midnight roads.
Enjoy your venison, forget the rest.

Spring Cleaning at Night

We know it is time:
accumulation taunts from the closets.
I bring out remnants — this dress
once danced under a blue moon in April.
Remember? What grew beneath its white folds
grows still in the dark between us.
I put it on and hear
the music that is left.
Outside a whippoorwill repeats, repeats.
We've had too much of beauty, I think,
and open the window anyway,
trying to hear something new.
The night inhabits us.
You toss me a sweatshirt from the pile
and it is winter ten years ago
in another house. And you move, surely,
as if you've done this all before.
You turn on the radio and we dance,
a man and a woman and our years
gathered around us like spectators.
The night spreads like your hand
on my shoulder.

Baptism

after "Baptism in Kansas," John Steuart Curry

Things keep going on the way they do
except one day in the middle of nothing
they don't.

I remember how hot it was — not a creak
from the windmill
and the Fords our folks had come in
steamed.

We stood around.
Our pockets were no place for hands,
they said, and wouldn't let us in the dark
of the barn or anywhere God wouldn't be
because the preacher was in the yard
to baptize whoever he could
in Tatums' water tank.

Six lined up.
I envied them the cool of their gowns
and the year or so they had on me
but not the way he dragged them under
and kept them there so long they bucked
like bullheads.

Mostly, I went along with the hymnbook
someone pushed at me
until he got to Ellen McGee,
held her under and didn't stop,
thinking maybe anything that pretty
was bound for goings on.

I was ready for something like the cat
I had tried to drown and failed
when up she came as sweet . . .
and stood for a spell at the edge
of the tank, at home in the sky.

And her gown, wet through, was true to her
and her face was where the sun had been.

1993

*From that sweating, heat-suffering
audience, I felt a kind of love.*
—*Norah Pollard*

Poems selected by Rennie McQuilkin

Featuring

James Merrill

Carole Stasiowski

Robert Cording

Norah Pollard

Bessy Reyna

Also read

Fresh Voices from Connecticut High Schools

164 East 72nd Street

These city apartment windows — my grandmother's once —
Must be replaced come Fall at great expense.
Pre-war sun shone through them on many a Saturday
Lunch unconsumed while frantic adolescence
Wheedled an old lady into hat and lipstick,
Into her mink, the taxi, the packed lobby,
Into our seats. Whereupon gold curtains parted
On Lakmé's silvery, not yet broken-hearted

Version of things as they were. But what remains
Exactly as it was except those panes?
Today's memo from the Tenants' Committee deplores
Even the ongoing deterioration
Of the widows in our building. Well. On the bright side,
Heating costs and street noise will be cut.
Sirens at present like intergalactic gay
Bars in full swing whoop past us night and day.

Sometimes, shocked wide awake, I've tried to reckon
How many lives — fifty, a hundred thousand? —
Are being shortened by that din of crosstown
Ruby flares, wherever blinds don't quite . . .
And shortened by how much? Ten minutes each?
Reaching the Emergency Room alive, the victim
Would still have to live years, just to repair
The sonic fallout of a single scare.

"Do you ever wonder where you'll — " Oh my dear,
Asleep somewhere, or at the wheel. Not here.
Within months of the bathroom ceiling's cave-in,
Which missed my grandmother by a white hair,
She moved back South. The point's to live in style,
Not to drop dead in it. On a carpet of flowers

Nine levels above ground, like Purgatory,
Our life is turning into a whole new story:

Juices, blue cornbread, afternoons at the gym —
Imagine who remembers how to swim!
Evenings of study, or intensive care
For one another. Early to bed. And later,
If the mirror's drowsy eye perceives a slight
But brilliant altercation between curtains
Healed by the leaden hand of — one of us?
A white-haired ghost? or the homunculus

A gentle alchemist behind them trains
To put in order these nocturnal scenes —
Two heads already featureless in gloom
Have fallen back to sleep. Tomorrow finds me
Contentedly playing peekaboo with a sylphlike
Quirk in the old glass, making the brickwork
On the street's far (bright) side ripple. Childhood's view.
My grandmother — an easy-to-see-through

Widow by the time she died — made it my own.
Bless her good sense. Far from those parts of town
Given to high finance, or the smash hit and steak house,
Macy's or crack, Saks or quick sex, this neighborhood
Saunters blandly forth, adjusting its clothing.
Things done in purple light before we met,
Uncultured things that twitched as on a slide
If thought about, fade like dreams. Two Upper East Side

Boys again! Rereading Sir Walter Scott
Or *Through the Looking Glass*, it's impossible not
To feel how adult life, with its storms and follies,
Is letting up, leaving me ten years old,
Trustful, inventive, once more good as gold
— And counting on this to help, should a new spasm
Wake the gray sleeper, or to improve his chances
When ceilings flush with unheard ambulances.

On Rollerblades

Wedded to road by a rack of wheels,
I feel its life rumble into my feet:
well-worn curve, pebbled approach,
silky patch of smooth asphalt,
rootcrack, frost heaves, they all
roll into me through the blades —
I who never skated as a child,
who meets the road now
wearing oversized sweats, fortified
with knee pads and wrist guards,
a weakened shin bandaged
against loss. Helmet snug around
all I remember and hope,
I take the lessons into blood and bone,
grateful for the muscle
that absorbs each shock and twist
and still propels forward
like the instinct to breathe. Soon
I've found a rhythm soothing and
hard, long-lined and fast,
motion beyond contradiction,

and I'm gathering steam
to claim the hill that has always
gummed legs and thickened lungs,
I'm struggling to stay with everything
rising ahead of me and in me,
legs plowing against a history
of defeat, but this time legs
don't falter, though they slow,
this time shoulders find the pitch
that cuts air, this time arms swing
to a beat almost forgotten, and as I

crest the hill I let the road take me
down the incline through the evergreens,
I ride gravity's lean trough, knees flexed
to every riffle in the road. I'm gliding
past the bandstand and softball field
when a voice breaks free —
it's mine! — do wah diddy-ing out loud,
legs and arms pumping to Manfred Mann,
and suddenly I imagine tank tops
in citrus hues, legs a mean silhouette,

so by the time I peel past the groundsmen
digging holes for a line of yews,
I'm sixteen and looking good,
strutting to Roy Orbison's sexual croon,
I'm laughing for all the rollicking inside,
waving to the kid on wobbly training wheels —
and now I'm gone, I'm not looking back,
I pound the road stoked on a memory:
a girl with bowl cut and faulted knees,
awkward in Simplicity — she cheers me on
squealing to see what we've become.

ROBERT CORDING

Kafka: Lilacs

Even yogurt diluted with water is too much
For him. Unable to swallow, he laughs

At the proofs he has been working on —
Hasn't he become his own Hunger Artist?

At arm's reach, a glass of beer, and pills
To numb the pain, both untouched. A clock

Replays the same hours and the sun
Arrives right on schedule, pausing now

At his window. It deepens the new greens
Of a tree where a bird's voice rises and falls,

Then settles at the sill, on which a vase
Of lilacs rests, their odors given out like light.

He thinks of how these last days, dying,
They have gone on drinking with such pleasure.

In the sunlight, their vase of water sparkles
Like a lake he swam in once with his father,

Each wave made light by sun and movement.
Then they drank beer at a cafe by the shore.

A bird kept reinventing its song. Leaves
Flashed white in the breeze off the water

And on the lake, far out, the single wing
Of a sailboat passed beyond an island,

As if from one realm into another.
And the colors — blues and greens, russet-browns

And creams. Tables of food. Cold beer he held
In his mouth and swallowed . . . When a friend

Wakes him, his room is trellised with blue shadows.
He shuts his eyes again, but there is no lake,

No breeze, no boat. There is only this late hour
And the spray of lilacs he opens his eyes to.

Everything is far and near at once, remote
As memory and yet present as these lilacs he takes

His time to relish, grateful for the way they fill
The room so completely with their rank sweetness.

He cannot eat, though when his friend offers
A bowl of strawberries, he breathes in their scent.

He cannot drink, but asks his friend to drink
For him, to wash down the taste of the fruit.

NORAH POLLARD

Wild Thing

I have long admired the heron
that stands for long hours in still water
not thinking of his career or the news,
but standing because he is a heron
and knows who he is and what a heron does.

And the great tiger that ate twelve people in Karachi
felt no guilt and licked the platter clean
because he was a tiger busy doing tiger things,
and nothing else needed to be explained.

The animals don't gripe about their in-laws
or deal with shrinks or engage in kinky sex
or change their spots or colors or their spouses,
they just do and do the thing they do the best.

My first time, in Eddie Gemza's pool with Eddie,
out under the stars and liquid as fish,
we played until he slipped it in without a warning,
so I bit his finger to the bone — he lost the tip.

And it was wild to see the blood torpedo the chlorine
and hear his swears and screams beneath the moon,
and it was wild to feel so wild and satisfied
to taste his blood and know just who I am.

Las Dos Camas

Ella tiene dos camas:
una es inmensa
       —y aún le falta espacio—
la otra es pequeñita
       —y aún le sobra espacio.

En la inmensa
los cuerpos se separan en la noche
como boxeadores al sonar la campana,
cada uno a su rincón.

En la pequeña
los cuerpos se entrelazan,
se amoldan,
se descubren,
se funden.

Dime como duermes
y te diré quién eres.

Two Beds

She has two beds:
one is huge
       —still she lacks the room—
the other is tiny
       —yet there's too much room.

In the huge bed,
bodies pull apart at night
like boxers at the sound of the bell,
each one to their own corner.

In the tiny one
bodies intertwine,
adapt to one another,
discover one another,
merge.

.

Tell me how you sleep
and I'll tell you who you are.

1994

*Festival director Rennie McQuilkin
takes care of poets better than anyone I've ever met.*
— Theodore Deppe

Poems selected by Ravi Shankar

Featuring

Richard Wilbur

Kate Rushin

Honor Moore

Martín Espada

Theodore Deppe

A Barred Owl

The warping night air having brought the boom
Of an owl's voice into her darkened room,
We tell the wakened child that all she heard
Was an odd question from a forest bird,
Asking of us, if rightly listened to,
"Who cooks for you?" and then "Who cooks for you?"

Words, which can make our terrors bravely clear,
Can also thus domesticate a fear,
And send a small child back to sleep at night
Not listening for the sound of stealthy flight
Or dreaming of some small thing in a claw
Borne up to some dark branch and eaten raw.

The Black Back-Ups

This is dedicated to Merry Clayton, Fontella Bass, Vonetta
Washington, Carolyn Franklin, Yolanda McCullough,
Carolyn Willis, Gwen Guthrie, Helaine Harris, and Darlene
Love. This is for all of the Black women who sang back-up for
Elvis Presley, John Denver, James Taylor, Lou Reed,
Etc. Etc. Etc.

I said Hey Babe
Take a Walk on the Wild Side
I said Hey Babe
Take a Walk on the Wild Side

And the colored girls say
Do dodo do do dodododo
Do dodo do do dodododo
Do dodo do do dodododo ooooo

This is for my Great-Grandmother Esther, my Grandmother
Addie, my grandmother called Sister, my Great-Aunt
Rachel, my Aunt Hilda, my Aunt tine, my Aunt Breda
my Aunt Gladys, my Aunt Helen, my Aunt Ellie,
my Cousin Barbara, my Cousin Dottie, and my Great-Great-
Aunt Vene.

This is dedicated to all of the Black women riding on buses
and subways back and forth to the Main Line, Haddonfield,
Cherry Hill, and Chevy Chase. This is for the women who
spend their summers in Rockport, Newport, Cape Cod, and
Camden, Maine. This is for the women who open those
bundles of dirty laundry sent home from those ivy-covered
campuses.

My Great-Aunt Rachel worked for the Carters
Ever since I can remember
There was *The Boy*
Whose name I never knew
And there was *The Girl*
Whose name was Jane

Great-Aunt Rachel brought Jane's dresses for me to wear
Perfectly Good Clothes
And I should've been glad to get them
Perfectly Good Clothes
No matter they didn't fit quite right
Perfectly Good Clothes
Brought home in a brown paper bag
With an air of accomplishment and excitement
Perfectly Good Clothes
Which I hated

At school
In Ohio
I swear to Gawd
There was always somebody
Telling me that the only person
In their whole house
Who listened and understood them
Despite the money and the lessons
Was the housekeeper
And I knew it was true
But what was I supposed to say

I know it's true
I watch her getting off the train
Moving slowly toward the Country Squire
With her uniform in her shopping bag
And the closer she gets to the car
The more the two little kids jump and laugh
And even the dog is about to
Turn inside out
Because they just can't wait until she gets there
Edna Edna   Wonderful Edna

But Aunt Edna to me, or Gram, or Miz Johnson or
Sister Johnson on Sundays

And the colored girls say
Do dodo do do dodododo
Do dodo do do dodododo
Do dodo do do dodododo ooooo

This is for Hattie McDaniel, Butterfly McQueen
Ethel Waters
Sapphire
Saphronia
Ruby Begonia
Aunt Jemima
Aunt Jemima on the Pancake Box

Aunt Jemima on the Pancake Box?
AuntJemimaonthepancakebox?
Ainchamamaonthepancakebox?
Ain't Chure Mama on the Pancake Box?

Mama Mama
Get off that box
And come home to me

And my Mama leaps off that box
She swoops down in her nurse's cape
Which she wears on Sunday
And for Wednesday night prayer meeting
And she wipes my forehead
And she fans my face
And she makes me a cup of tea
And it don't do a thing for my real pain
Except she is my Mama

Mama Mommy Mammy
Mam-mee Mam-mee
I'd Walk a Mill-yon Miles
For one of your smiles

This is for the Black Back-Ups
This is for my mama and your mama
My grandma and your grandma
This is for the thousand thousand million million
Black Back-Ups

And the colored girls say
Do dodo do do dodododo
do   dodo
  dodo
      do
        do

Shenandoah

Photograph: Breakfast after our first full night:
Elbow on the table, flat against your face, intent
   on the cup you look into. Your hair glints
     in three-year-old light.
In these rooms of borrowed furniture, white
walls, wide windows that curve, I have been solitary.
   A cymbedium orchid. Artichokes. Fresh
     trout. I tear pink netting from
the orchid, float it. Red wine is breathing. A plane
lands hours away, and I can think of you driving
   a valley roofed with clouds, your voice
     like the charge of new weather.

Yesterday, eyes shut, sun on my face, I could
remember you viscerally: Heat, sun that caressed
   our naked skin, blond grasses, weeds baked
       to vivid rust. There was no
snow — odd that far north in late October. From ours
other mountains were feathery with bare trees
   and some phenomenon of light turned
      their billowing crests
lavender. See those mountains make a giant sprawled
on her back: those, breasts; the one called Otter, torso.
   See the lake bright near her cheek, the
     trout stream etch her chin.

I am afraid in the vestibule, your face
smiling its guileless welcome. I want to cry, hold you,
   open through your breasts into safe billowing
     darkness. I kiss you
as if we are just friends. I lead you through
white rooms. I hand you the orchid because I cannot
tell you. You reach. I start, as if your touch were

too much light. I trim
the artichokes. The red wind breathes. I must cover
the curved window. In this valley roofed with clouds, I live
        alone in rooms on a street where
              all the shades are pulled.

We drink red wine. We unbutton, touch. We eat
trout — clouded eye, clear black night shut from the house, petal
   flush of your skin. We eat artichokes, mark
        leaf after leaf with our teeth.
The orchid floats. It is your darkness I want with my
mouth. If I could speak as sound not edged into
   word, I could tell you. Leaves now: two, four,
              five at once. We reach
center, loose lavender-streaked swirl, split the naked
heart in the night bed where I speak with my hands
   and we breathe, mouth to mouth, unedged,
              shorn to simple tenderness.

MARTÍN ESPADA

The Other Alamo

San Antonio, Texas, 1990

In the Crockett Hotel dining room,
a chalk-faced man in medaled uniform
growls a prayer
at the head of the veterans' table.
Throughout the map of this saint-hungry city,
hands strain for the touch of shrines,
genuflection before cannon and memorial plaque,
grasping the talisman of Bowie knife replica
at the souvenir shop, visitors
in white biblical quote T-shirts.

40

The stones in the walls are smaller
than the fists of Texas martyrs;
their cavernous mouths could drink the canal to mud.
The Daughters of the Republic
print brochures dancing with Mexican demons,
Santa Anna's leg still hopping
to conjunto accordions.
The lawyers who conquered farmland
by scratching on parchment in an oil lamp haze,
the cotton growers who kept the time
of Mexican peasant lives dangling from their watch chains,
the vigilantes hooded like blind angels
hunting with torches for men the color of night,
gathering at church, the capitol, or the porch
for a century all said this: *Alamo*.

In 1949, three boys
in Air Force dress khaki
ignored the whites-only sign
at the diner by the bus station:
A soldier from Baltimore, who heard *nigger* sung here
more often than his name, but would not glance away;
another blond and solemn as his Tennessee of whitewashed spires;
another from distant Puerto Rico, cap tipped at an angle
in a country where brown skin
could be boiled for the leather of a vigilante's wallet.

The waitress squinted a glare and refused their contamination,
the manager lost his crewcut politeness
and blustered about local customs,
the police, with surrounding faces,
jeered about tacos and señoritas
on the Mexican side of town.

We're not leaving, they said,
and hunched at their stools
till the manager ordered the cook,
sweat-burnished black man unable to hide his grin,

to slide cheeseburgers on plates
across the counter.
We're not hungry, they said,
and left a week's pay for the cook.
One was my father; his word for fury
is Texas.

This afternoon, the heat clouds the air like bothered gnats.
The lunch counter was wrecked for the dump years ago.
In the newspapers, a report of vandals
scarring the wooden doors
of the Alamo
in black streaks of fire.

TED DEPPE

The Book of God

I'm thinking tonight of the three times
Marisol's tried to kill herself before her sixth birthday —
long red suture lines on both arms —
and of the picture she tore from the *Newsweek*
I'd brought to read on break — I still don't know

how she got it — a photo of a crucified girl,
one of several Bosnian children nailed to the doors
of their own homes to frighten the parents away.
For Marisol, she hangs there without explanation,
head bent down, black hair falling over jutting ribs.

The single spike through her blue feet
rotates her legs inward, creating a knock-kneed
pigeon-toed schoolgirl of a saint.
Around the tormented girl Marisol taped whole tulips
from the hospital garden. Sacrilege my taking down

her bedside shrine. Nothing I said about the photo
troubling the other children made sense:
when I took the picture from her wall she dug
her nails in my wrist, tried to bite my hand.
Only later, and reluctantly, she accepted

the notepad I gave her to write about the girl.
She didn't want words inside but on the cover
she wrote in block letters THE BOOK OF GOD
CAME BACK AS A SMALL GIRL.
On each page she drew pictures she couldn't talk about.

1995

It was an extraordinary occasion for me — my
first reading after my wife Jane Kenyon's death — and a
challenge getting out of the parking lot afterward.
— Donald Hall

Poems selected by Steve Foley

Featuring

Galway Kinnell

Cheryl Savageau

Jeffrey Harrison

Sue Ellen Thompson

Patricia Smith

Donald Hall

Also read

Fresh Voices from Connecticut High Schools

How Could She Not

In Memory of Jane Kenyon, 1947–1995

The air glitters. Overfull clouds
slide across the sky. A short shower,
its parallel diagonals visible
against the firs, douses and then
refreshes the crocuses. We knew
it might happen one day this week.
Out the open door, east of us, stand
the mountains of New Hampshire.
There, too, the sun is bright,
and heaped cumuli make their shadowy
ways along the horizon. When we learn
that she died this morning, we wish
we could think: how could it not
have been today? In another room,
Kiri Te Kanawa is singing
Mozart's *Laudate Dominum*
from far in the past, her voice
barely there over the swishing of scythes,
and rattlings of horse-pulled
mowing machines dragging
their cutter bar's little reciprocating
triangles through the timothy.

This morning did she wake
in the dark, almost used up
by her year of pain? By first light
did she glimpse the world
as she had loved it, and see
that if she died now, she would
be leaving him in a day like paradise?
Near sunrise did her hold loosen a little?

Having these last days spoken
her whole heart to him, who spoke
his whole heart to her, might she not
have felt that in the silence to come
he would not feel any word
was missing? When her room filled
with daylight, how could she not
have slipped under a spell, with him
next to her, his arms around her, as they
had been, it may then have seemed,
all her life? How could she not
press her cheek to his cheek,
which presses itself to hers
from now on? How could she not
rise and go, with sunlight at the window,
and the drone, fading, deepening, hard to say,
of a single-engine plane in the distance,
coming for her, that no one else hears?

CHERYL SAVAGEAU

First Grade — Standing in the Hall

for my brother, Ed

Because he can't read
the teacher makes him stand
in the hall. He can sing
all his letters, knows
what they look like. He knows
that out of books come stories,
like the ones his Gramma told him.
Now she is in the hospital.
He wonders if she is sleeping,
when she will come home.

The letters do not
talk to him.
They keep their stories
to themselves.

He is hopeless, he is stupid,
he is standing in the hall.
He is waiting in the hall
for the principal
to see him, for the bell to ring,
for the teacher
to call him back inside.

After awhile
when no one comes
he stops crying.
A spider is webbing
the pie-shaped window pane,
and outside,
the sun is making fire
in the yellow leaves.

If he listens closely
a song will begin in him
that the teachers
can't silence.

JEFFREY HARRISON

Totem

We had to rip a few boards
of the soffit off to fit
the new front door into place,
and when we stopped for lunch I stood
on a picnic bench and stuck

my head up through the opening,
into the stuffy darkness there
below the eaves and, as my eyes
adjusted, made it out—was that . . .
a canoe paddle!—its wood
still golden under the varnish
when I pulled it into daylight
despite how many years
of lying completely enclosed
in that wedge of stale dark air.
That paddle had us baffled
until my mother remembered,
or thought she remembered, hearing
somewhere of a superstition
about a paddle in the roof
bringing good luck. The whole family
was there, as I remember,
standing on the cabin's porch,
and we passed the paddle from one
to another in amused wonder,
each member examining it
as if it were a talisman
or fetish and we were taking part
unwittingly in some ancient
but spontaneous ritual—
which is what it might have looked like
to anyone paddling by
on the lake below. At first
we wanted to keep it, but then
the fear of what dark current might
overtake our lives, an undertow
we were just beginning to feel,
outweighed the temptation to hang it
with the others in the boathouse.
So we slipped it through the hole
we'd made before nailing the boards
back where they belonged, closing it
in again, carrying on

the superstition or creating
a new one: a perfectly good
canoe paddle several feet
above our heads, steering us
through difficult passages
and blessing us each time
we pass underneath it,
going in or out the door.

SUE ELLEN THOMPSON

Terms of Endearment

Sweet biscuit of my life,
I've been thinking of your smile
and how I'd steal a little bite
of it if you were here; of the delights

I've known in the alleyway between
the whitewashed storefronts of your teeth;
of how I've pressed one smithereen
after another of mille-feuille, mousseline

of late-night conversation upon your lips,
forever poised at the brink of kissdom,
their slightest sigh enough to lift
a tableskirt. Perfectest pumpkin

in the patch, your heft on mine
is what I crave, your brows so fine
I could not carve them with a steak knife.
You have the acorn eyes

of the football season, the ass
of an autumn afternoon, of boys en masse
in soccer shorts. Yours is the vast
contained candescence of a Titian under glass,

it is the gold leaf laid
by February sun, the lemonade's
pale wash in August. Should you fade,
like sun on windowsills crocheted

with shadow, then suddenly gone dark,
your face will leave its watermark
upon this page, which is already part
of love's confection, our little work of art.

PATRICIA SMITH

Undertaker

When a bullet enters the brain, the head explodes.
I can think of no softer warning for the mothers
who sit doubled before my desk,
knotting their smooth brown hands,
and begging, Fix my boy, fix my boy.
Here's his high school picture.
And the smirking, mildly mustachioed player
in the crinkled snapshot
looks nothing like the plastic bag of boy
stored and dated in the cold room downstairs.
In the picture, he is cocky and chiseled,
clutching the world by the balls. I know the look.
Now he is flaps of cheek,
slivers of jawbone, a surprised eye,
assorted teeth, bloody tufts of napped hair.
The building blocks of my business.
So I swallow hard, turn the photo face down
and talk numbers instead. The high price
of miracles startles the still-young woman,
but she is prepared. I know that she has sold
everything she owns, that cousins and uncles
have emptied their empty bank accounts,

that she dreams of her baby
in tuxedoed satin, flawless in an open casket,
a cross or blood red rose tacked to his fingers,
his halo set at a cocky angle.
I write a figure on a piece of paper
and push it across to her
while her chest heaves with hoping.
She stares at the number, pulls in
a slow weepy breath: Jesus.

But Jesus isn't on my payroll. I work alone
until the dim insistence of morning,
bent over my grisly puzzle pieces, gluing,
stitching, creating a chin with a brushstroke,
I plop glass eyes into rigid sockets,
then carve eyelids from a forearm, an inner thigh,
I plump shattered skulls, and paint the skin
to suggest warmth, an impending breath.
I reach into collapsed cavities to rescue
a tongue, an ear. Lips are never easy to recreate.
And I try not to remember the stories,
the tales the mothers must bring me
to ease their own hearts. Oh, they cry,
my Ronnie, my Willie, my Michael, my Chico.
It was self-defense. He was on his way home,
a dark car slowed down, they must have thought
he was someone else. He stepped between
two warring gang members at a party.
Really, he was trying to get off the streets,
trying to pull away from the crowd.
He was trying to help a friend.
He was in the wrong place at the wrong time.
Fix my boy; he was a good boy. Make him the way he was.

But I have explored the jagged gaps
in the boy's body, smoothed the angry edges
of bullet-holes. I have touched him in places
no mother knows, and I have birthed

his new face. I know that he believed himself
invincible, that he most likely hissed
Fuck you, man! before the bullets lifted him
off his feet. I try not to imagine
his swagger, his lizard-lidded gaze,
his young mother screaming into the phone.
She says she will find the money, and I know
this is the truth that fuels her, forces her
to place one foot in front of the other.

Suddenly, I want to take her down
to the chilly room, open the bag
and shake its terrible bounty onto the
gleaming steel table. I want her to see him, to touch him,
to press her lips to the flap of cheek.
The woman needs to wither, finally, and move on.
We both jump as the phone rattles in its hook.
I pray that it's my wife, a bill collector, a wrong number.
But the wide, questioning silence on the other end
is too familiar. Another mother needing a miracle.
Another homeboy coming home.

DONALD HALL

Without

we lived in a small island stone nation
without color under gray clouds and wind
distant the unlimited ocean acute
lymphoblastic leukemia without seagulls
or palm trees without vegetation
or animal life only barnacles and lead
colored moss that darkened when months did

hours days weeks months weeks days hours
the year endured without punctuation

february without ice winter sleet
snow melted recovered but nothing
without thaw although cold streams hurtled
no snowdrop or crocus rose no yellow
no red leaves of maple without october

no spring no summer no autumn no winter
no rain no peony thunder no woodthrush
the book was a thousand pages without commas
without mice oak leaves windstorms
no castles no plazas no flags no parrots
without carnival or the procession of relics
intolerable without brackets or colons

silence without color sound without smell
without apples without pork to rupture gnash
unpunctuated without churches uninterrupted
no orioles ginger noses no opera no
without fingers daffodils cheekbones
the body was a nation a tribe dug into stone
assaulted white blood broken to shards

provinces invaded bombed shot shelled
artillery sniper fire helicopter gunship
grenade burning murder landmine starvation
the ceasefire lasted forty-eight hours
then a shell exploded in a market
pain vomit neuropathy morphine nightmare
confusion the rack terror the vise

vincristine ara-c cytoxan vp-16
loss of memory loss of language losses
pneumocystis carinii pneumonia bactrim
foamless unmitigated sea without sea
delirium whipmarks of petechiae
multiple blisters of herpes zoster
and how are you doing today I am doing

one afternoon say the sun came out
moss took on greenishness leaves fell
the market opened a loaf of bread a sparrow
a bony dog wandered back sniffing a lath
it might be possible to take up a pencil
unwritten stanzas taken up and touched
beautiful terrible sentences unuttered

the sea unrelenting wave gray the sea
flotsam without islands broken crates
block after block the same house the mall
no cathedral no hobo jungle the same women
and men they longed to drink hayfields no
without dog or semicolon or village square
without monkey or lily without garlic

1996

The best for me was performing my
"Thus Far By Faith" with Tim Moran and Kent Hewitt
who composed the music. It was wonderful.
— Marilyn Nelson

Poems selected by Robert Cording

Featuring

Stanley Kunitz

Sharon Olds

Brendan Galvin

Marge Piercy

Marilyn Nelson

Also read

Fresh Voices from Connecticut High Schools

Touch Me

Summer is late, my heart.
Words plucked out of the air
some forty years ago
when I was wild with love
and torn almost in two
scatter like leaves this night
of whistling wind and rain.
It is my heart that's late,
it is my song that's flown.
Outdoors all afternoon
under a gunmetal sky
staking my garden down,
I kneeled to the crickets trilling
underfoot as if about
to burst from their crusty shells;
and like a child again
marveled to hear so clear
and brave a music pour
from such a small machine.
What makes the engine go?
Desire, desire, desire.
The longing for the dance
stirs in the buried life.
One season only,
      and it's done.
So let the battered old willow
thrash against the windowpanes
and the house timbers creak.
Darling, do you remember
the man you married? Touch me,
remind me who I am.

Mrs. Krikorian

She saved me. When I arrived in 6th grade,
a known criminal, the new teacher
asked me to stay after school the first day, she said
I've heard about you. She was a tall woman,
with a deep crevice between her breasts,
and a large, calm nose. She said,
This is a special library pass.
As soon as you finish your hour's work —
that hour's work that took ten minutes
and then the devil glanced into the room
and found me empty, a house standing open —
you can go to the library. Every hour
I'd zip through the work in a dash and slip out of my
seat as if out of God's side and sail
down to the library, solo through the empty
powerful halls, flash my pass
and stroll over to the dictionary
to look up the most interesting word
I knew, *spank*, dipping two fingers
into the jar of library paste to
suck that tart mucilage as I
came to the page with the cocker spaniel's
silks curling up like the fine steam of the body.
After *spank*, and *breast*, I'd move on
to *Abe Lincoln* and *Helen Keller*,
safe in their goodness till the bell, thanks
to Mrs. Krikorian, amiable giantess
with the kind eyes. When she asked me to write
a play, and direct it, and it was a flop, and I
hid in the coat-closet, she brought me a candy-cane
as you lay a peppermint on the tongue, and the worm
will come up out of the bowel to get it.
And so I was emptied of Lucifer

and filled with school glue and eros and
Amelia Earhart, saved by Mrs. Krikorian.
And who had saved Mrs. Krikorian?
When the Turks came across Armenia, who
slid her into the belly of a quilt, who
locked her in a chest, who mailed her to America?
And *that* one, who saved *her*, and *that* one—
who saved *her*, to save the one
who saved Mrs. Krikorian, who was
standing there on the sill of 6th grade, a
wide-hipped angel, smokey hair
standing up weightless all around her head?
I end up owing my soul to so many,
to the Armenian nation, one more soul someone
jammed behind a stove, drove
deep into a crack in a wall,
shoved under a bed. I would wake
up, in the morning, under my bed—not
knowing how I had got there—and lie
in the dusk, the dustballs beside my face
round and ashen, shining slightly
with the eerie comfort of what is neither good nor evil.

BRENDAN GALVIN

For a Little Girl of Pompeii

The dog's still jerking on his chain
because the slaves knew life comes
before duty. They are still running
from the sleepy forenoon
you've slept away for nineteen centuries.

Your rib cage got to me,
and your hands gathered before you
in a prayer to falling ash

or in the simple lifting of your tunic
to your face: a little girl asleep on her side.

It looks like there's a flower
growing nearby, but I'm not going to pluck
that consolation for you. Instead,
I'm going to make believe
you're real as this bad photo
makes you seem, not just technician's plaster
blown into the hollow where you were.

Real as graffiti on those walls, "Samius
to Cornelius, go hang yourself,"
real as the umbrella
Vesuvius opened above your head.

It's been worse. Pits
have been uncovered where you're multiplied
millions of times, not just in dreams,
not just by acts of random providence.

You're realer there than patios
the Prince d'Elbeuf
lifted from your marble town
because you're utterly without protection.

It's your ribs that get me,
moreso your hands in their small gesture.
I have one hand for my daughter, crossing streets,
but sometimes, from now on,
I'm going to make believe my other hand's
for you. To give me balance.
Between the two of you, you two could lift me.

The cat's song

Mine, says the cat, putting out his paw of darkness.
My lover, my friend, my slave, my toy, says
the cat making on your chest his gesture of drawing
milk from his mother's forgotten breasts.

Let us walk in the woods, says the cat.
I'll teach you to read the tabloid of scents,
to fade into shadow, wait like a trap, to hunt.
Now I lay this plump warm mouse on your mat.

You feed me, I try to feed you, we are friends,
says the cat, although I am superior to you.
Can you leap twenty times the height of your body?
Can you run up and down trees? Jump between roofs?

Let us rub our bodies together and talk of touch.
My emotions are pure as salt crystals and as hard.
My lusts glow like my eyes. I sing to you in the mornings
walking round and round your bed and into your face.

Come I will teach you to dance as naturally
as falling asleep and waking and stretching long, long.
I speak greed with my paws and fear with my whiskers.
Envy lashes my tail. Love speaks me entire, a word

of fur. I will teach you to be still as an egg
and to slip like the ghost of wind through the grass.

Abba Jacob and Miracles

One day Abba Jacob
was praying in a sunbeam
by the door to his underground cell,
and the brethren came to him
to ask him about miracles.
One of the elders said,
My mother's spirit came back
and turned out all the lights
the night we gathered for her wake:
Was that a miracle?
Another said, One spring evening
a white rainbow of mist
passed over our heads:
Was that a miracle?
They went on like this
for several hours.
Abba Jacob listened.
Then there was silence.

Big deal,
said Abba Jacob.
Miracles happen all the time.
We're here
aren't we?

1997

*It was largest audience I had ever read for, but when
the light and faces faded, I relaxed because I was now reading
only to the dark and maybe 7,000 crickets.*
— Billy Collins

Poems selected by Kate Rushin

Featuring

Mark Doty

Patricia Smith

Dick Allen

Naomi Ayala

Billy Collins

Visitation

When I heard he had entered the harbor,
and circled the wharf for days,
I expected the worst: shallow water,

confusion, some accident to bring
the young humpback to grief.
Don't they depend on a compass

lodged in the salt-flooded folds
of the brain, some delicate
musical mechanism to navigate

their true course? How many ways,
in our century's late iron hours,
might we have led him to disaster?

That, in those days, was how
I'd come to see the world:
dark upon dark, any sense

of spirit an embattled flame
sparked against wind-driven rain
till pain snuffed it out. I thought,

This is what experience gives us,
and I moved carefully through my life
while I waited . . . Enough,

it wasn't that way at all. The whale
—exuberant, proud maybe, playful,
like the early music of Beethoven—

cruised the footings for smelts
clustered near the pylons
in mercury flocks. He

(do I have the gender right?)
would negotiate the rusty hulls
of the Portuguese fishing boats

—*Holy Infant, Little Marie*—
with what could only be read
as pleasure, coming close

then diving, trailing on the surface
big spreading circles
until he'd breach, thrilling us

with the release of pressured breath,
and the bulk of his sleek young head
—a wet black leather sofa

already barnacled with ghostly lice—
and his elegant and unlikely mouth,
and the marvelous afterthought of the flukes,

and the way his broad flippers
resembled a pair of clownish gloves
or puppet hands, looming greenish white

beneath the bay's clouded sheen.
When he had consumed his pleasure
of the shimmering swarm, his pleasure, perhaps,

in his own admired performance,
he swam out the harbor mouth,
into the Atlantic. And though grief

has seemed to me itself a dim,
salt suspension in which I've moved,
blind thing, day by day,

through the wreckage, barely aware
of what I stumbled toward, even I
couldn't help but look

at the way this immense figure
graces the dark medium,
and shines so: heaviness

which is no burden to itself.
What did you think, that joy
was some slight thing?

PATRICIA SMITH

Sweet Daddy

62. You would have been 62.
I would have given you a Roosevelt Road kinda time,
an all-night jam in a twine-time joint,
where you could have taken over the mike
and crooned a couple.

The place be all blue light
and JB air
and big-legged women
giggling at the way
you spit tobacco into the sound system,
showing up some dime-store howler
with his pink car
pulled right up to the door outside.

You would have been 62.
And the smoke would have bounced
right off the top of your head
like good preachin'.
I can see you now, twirling those thin hips,

growling 'bout if it wasn't for bad luck
you wouldn't have no luck at all.
I said —
wasn't for bad luck,
no luck at all.

Nobody ever accused you
of walking the paradise line.
You could suck Luckies
and line your mind with rubbing alcohol
if that's what the night called for,
but Lord, you could cry foul
while B.B. growled Lucille from the jukebox,
you could dance like killing roaches
and kiss those downsouth ladies
on fatback mouths, *Ooooweee*, they'd say,
that sweet man sho' knows how deep my well goes.
And I bet you did, daddy,
I bet you did.

But hey, here's to just another number —
to a man who wrote poems
on the back of cocktail napkins
and brought them home to his daughter
who'd written her rhymes
under the cover of blankets.
Here's to a strain on the caseload.
Here's to the fat bullet
that left its warm chamber
to find you.
Here's to the miracles
that spilled from your head
and melted into the air
like jazz.

The carpet had to be destroyed.
And your collected works

on aging, yellowed twists of napkin
can't bring you back.
B.B. wail and blue Lucille
can't bring you back.
A daughter who grew to write screams
can't bring you back.

But a room
just like this one,
which suddenly seems to fill
with the dread odors of whiskey and smoke,
can bring you here
as close as my breathing.

But the moment is hollow.
It stinks.
It stinks sweet.

DICK ALLEN

Backstroking at Thrushwood Lake

Momentary beds of white burst flowers
   Appear behind us. Kicking and pulling,
We continually create what disappears,
   So keep from drowning.
And what a sky is overhead! Great medieval blurs
   Of cumulus ascending.

We reenact da Vinci's naked man
   With four arms, four legs, fingertips
And feet in square and circle to explain
   Proportion. Or imagine hips
Rocking in a snowfield: we have lain
   Down in snow, and left snow angel trails

From one side to the other, or a vertical
   String of paper dolls, joined head to toe across
Still waters. If we yell
   Out for the joy of it, or toss
Our heads from side to side, this spell
   Is exultation, just as it is madness.

Our elemental madness — that we know we live
   Today, this century, this year, this hour, minute
Everything is happening. Above,
   A flock of geese goes flying down towards Bridgeport.
Emerging in a high and cloudy cave,
   A Boeing's shadow is a crosslike print

To which you raise your head. The shore
   Is sand and willows — and our children
Floating near it, bobbing heads and figures
   Flattened on their plastic rafts. The wind
Blows them toward each other;
   Or away, unless they link their hands

While we tread water. Look at them. Their moments
   Also disappear, yet last — the paradox
of memory. Think of mullein weeds,
   Full and empty pods upon their stalks,
Dead flowers and the living seeds,
   The washcloth texture of their flannel leaves,

And turn around. Stay close to me. Leave froth
   Again behind us and to both our sides.
Nothing ever will be beautiful enough
   Unless we're satisfied with how we ride
Waves backward and can love,
   For what we fashion, though we cannot keep, we need —

As I, these living moments, need the lake against
   My back, those towers in the clouds, the cries
Of children linking hands, the houses fenced

About the lake, their windows brimmed with sky
Blue and white — trapped in the way your glance
  Catches me, and holds me, and all meanings fly.

NAOMI AYALA

El Placer de la Palabra

The pleasure of your speaking.
The loud rivers
of your speaking. The soft, bending
arch of recognition
between your smile & the speed of busy
hands at the salary of a cab,
bus, in the restaurant
of our millionaire ambition
minimum-waged into this narrow,
small-breathing dream
we call a golden country.
Azúcar
negra. Brown sugar. *Te quiero*. I love
your speaking. I go
with loving rhythm
through the revolving
door of days spent moving
without moving. I find you & my ear
is a blackhole for the music
of your dancing tongue.
My body is a blackhole.
If I carry *home* on my back —
crawling into foxholes,
into the safeway of night —
when I pass you carrying all you have
on your own hardened back, your words
bring the cool sweat to the heat
of my daily life. And I stop

to court you, *azúcar*
negra, brown sugar, your tongue,
to drink of your crystal
clear music.

BILLY COLLINS

Japan

Today I pass the time reading
a favorite haiku,
saying the few words over and over.

It feels like eating
the same small, perfect grape
again and again.

I walk through the house reciting it
and leave its letters falling
through the air of every room.

I stand by the big silence of the piano and say it.
I say it in front of a painting of the sea.
I tap out its rhythm on an empty shelf.

I listen to myself saying it,
then I say it without listening,
then I hear it without saying it.

And when the dog looks up at me,
I kneel down on the floor
and whisper it into each of his long white ears.

It's the one about the one-ton temple bell
with the moth sleeping on its surface,

and every time I say it, I feel the excruciating
pressure of the moth
on the surface of the iron bell.

When I say it at the window,
the bell is the world
and I am the moth resting there.

When I say it at the mirror,
I am the heavy bell
and the moth is life with its papery wings.

And later, when I say it to you in the dark,
you are the bell,
and I am the tongue of the bell, ringing you,

and the moth has flown
from its line
and moves like a hinge in the air above our bed.

1998

A beautiful evening, the lawn filled, and in the audience
a cousin I hadn't seen in years, not a poet but a practicing dentist,
at ease in a place where so many come to hear poetry.
—*Carolyn Forché*

Poems selected by Pit Menousek Pinegar

Featuring

Carolyn Forché

Natasha Trethewey

Margaret Gibson

Leo Connellan

Hayden Carruth

Lucille Clifton

Curfew

for Sean

The curfew was as long as anyone could remember
Certainty's tent was pulled from its little stakes
It was better not to speak any language
There was a man cloaked in doves, there was chandelier music
The city, translucent, shattered but did not disappear
Between the no-longer and the still to come
The child asked if the bones in the wall
Belonged to the lights in the tunnel
Yes, I said, and the stars nailed shut his heaven

His Hands

His hands will never be large enough.
Not for the woman who sees in his face
the father she can't remember,
or her first husband, the soldier with two wives—
all the men who would only take.
Not large enough to deflect
the sharp edges of her words.

Still he tries to prove himself in work,
his callused hands heaving crates
all day on the docks, his pay twice spent.
He brings home what he can, buckets of crabs
from his morning traps, a few green bananas.

His supper waits in the warming oven,
the kitchen dark, the screens hooked.
He thinks, *make the hands gentle*
as he raps lightly on the back door.
He has never had a key.

Putting her hands to his, she pulls him in,
sets him by the stove. Slowly, she rubs oil
into his cracked palms, drawing out soreness
from the swells, removing splinters, taking
whatever his hands will give.

MARGARET GIBSON

Prayer Ascending, Prayer Descending

God, let me be a sensual
hush, wind
that ripples the olive
leaves, nests
in the lush frangipani, its blossoms
scattered, crushed beneath my sandals,

lifting into flowerwine and gravid scent —

for whatever I know of source
and ascent,
blossoming forth,
lies rooted in the backyard plum tree
I climbed one summer night,
no more than eight,
and no one, least
I, knew what I climbed down from,

ripe with secrets
I want to have a word for now —

as if night sky and years of light
could be so
easily swallowed,

eaten, owned —

God, like a plum.

Or, if not hushed, then taut and thrummed,
as, lightly at mass, *el domingo pasado,*
los guitarras. Listening,

I took the host,
the solar disk
into my mouth,
I swallowed the sun —
this is my body,

and beneath what Spanish I knew,
the tree of blood inside me
shimmered down to the oldest prayer,
Maya Quiche —
Pardon my sins, God Earth,
I am becoming, for a moment,
Your breath, and also your body.

LEO CONNELLAN

Shooter

Hey Momma I'm going to know Brooklyn
just because we live here. Nothing's happening,
dying is living, so we drive by and shoot because
nothing is ours, you don't destroy yours.
Sometimes we hit and sometimes we get hit. A
bullet just rolled off my roof. You go to

Columbia University, I go to the undertaker.
I explain the bullet I keep on my dresser to
my momma she worry more than she already
thinkabout . . . so don't tell her I'll be here
until I'm not . . . oh, Momma you birthed us abandoned
by men, any man, a couple of steady sleepovers who
could buy shoes, food, clothes to keep coming. You
did what you could for us and now all you got
for it is headstones.

HAYDEN CARRUTH

Scrambled Eggs and Whiskey

Scrambled eggs and whiskey
in the false-dawn light. Chicago,
a sweet town, bleak, God knows,
but sweet. Sometimes. And
weren't we fine tonight?
When Hank set up that limping
treble roll behind me
my horn just growled and I
thought my heart would burst.
And Brad M. pressing with the
soft stick and Joe-Anne
singing low. Here we are now
in the White Tower, leaning
on one another, too tired
to go home. But don't say a word,
don't tell a soul, they wouldn't
understand, they couldn't, never
in a million years, how fine,
how magnificent we were
in that old club tonight.

the thirty eighth year

the thirty eighth year
of my life,
plain as bread
round as a cake
an ordinary woman.

an ordinary woman.

i had expected to be
smaller than this,
more beautiful,
wiser in afrikan ways,
more confident,
i had expected
more than this.

i will be forty soon.
my mother once was forty.

my mother died at forty four,
a woman of sad countenance
leaving behind a girl
awkward as a stork.
my mother was thick,
her hair was a jungle and
she was very wise
and beautiful
and sad.

i have dreamed dreams
for you mama
more than once.
i have wrapped me in your skin
and made you live again

more than once.
i have taken the bones you hardened
and built daughters
and they blossom and promise fruit
like afrikan trees.
i am a woman now.
an ordinary woman.
in the thirty eighth
year of my life,
surrounded by life,
a perfect picture of
blackness blessed,
i had not expected this
loneliness.

if it is western,
if it is the final
europe in my mind,
if in the middle of my life
i am turning the final turn
into the shining dark
let me come to it whole
and holy
not afraid
not lonely
out of mother's life
into my own.
into my own.

i had expected more than this.
i had not expected to be
an ordinary woman.

1999

*The whole evening is poetry: the poetry of
human words, the poetry of sky and earth, the poetry
of making connection between soul and soul.*
— *Joy Harjo*

Poems selected by Ginny Lowe Connors

Featuring

Eamon Grennan

Gray Jacobik

Stephen Dunn

Joy Harjo

Billy Collins

Wing Road

Amazing —
how the young man who empties our dustbin
ascends the truck as it moves
away from him, rises up like an angel
in a china-blue check shirt and lilac
woollen cap, dirty work-gloves, rowanberry
red bandanna flapping at his throat. He plants
one foot above the mudguard, locks
his left hand to a steel bar
stemming from the dumper's loud mouth,
and is borne away, light as a cat, right leg
dangling, the dazzled air snatching at that black-
bearded face. He breaks to a smile, leans wide
and takes the morning to his puffed chest —
right arm stretched far out,
a checkered china-blue wing
gliding between blurred earth
and heaven, a messenger under the locust trees
that stand in silent panic at his passage. But
his mission is not among the trees:
he has flanked both sunlit rims of Wing Road
with empty dustbins, each lying on its side,
its battered lid fallen beside it, each
letting noonlight scour its emptiness
to shining. Carried off in a sudden cloud
of diesel smoke, in a woeful crying out
of brakes and gears, a roaring of monstrous
mechanical appetite, he has left this unlikely radiance
straggled behind him, where the crows —
covening in branches — will flash and haggle.

"Every man whose soul is not a clod hath visions"

from Keats, "The Fall of Hyperion"

Between Taylorville and Mattoon, along a flat
numbered country road, hundreds of martin houses,
hotels, motels, apartment buildings, some carved
out of gourds, but most plywood, cut, assembled
and painted to resemble their larger counterparts,
except for the circled entrances and *porches*
the farmer called them. Working at it nearly
thirty years he said. His kids and grandkids
made some, and folks were always dropping by
with homemade or rescued additions. Vacant usually,
wind-blown as all else on that open prairie,
a town atop poles and hung from trees, strung
along a propped-up beam that ran from milk barn
to hay barn, another from hay barn to tractor barn.
Several accommodations bowed an old clothesline.
Gives you something to look forward to, he said,
those first weeks in April when everyone's moved
in and it's noisy as hell. Each year there's a dozen
or so circling about that can't find a vacancy —
means I've got building to do after the corn's siloed.
He was squirrelly, sunburnt, a bit of a sprite,
one of those husky compact men who have always
stewarded land. Countless times I've thought of
his town for purple martins, fully aloft, swinging
unvisited in snow or the torrential thunderstorms
that rage through that place, motionless, cracking
in August heat, and thought too, of those clamorous
weeks, every household chirping and settling
at nightfall, rousing itself before dawn, the moiré
against fields and clouds as the martins alternate
quick flaps and glides, spread tails and fan-out

over farmland, rise and sink as currents move.
The peal of silence the day they leave. A serious
man's serious folly invented to serve his mind
and spirit as folly will—excessive, redemptive,
preposterous, the glory of the overdone anyone
of us is capable of, yet usually avoids—and
one thing more for him through the long months
of fallow fields: a wild domesticity drawing near.

STEPHEN DUNN

Imagining Myself My Father

I drove slowly, the windows open,
letting the emptiness within meet
the brotherly emptiness without.
Deer grazed by the Parkway's edge,
solemnly enjoying their ridiculous,
gentle lives. There were early signs
of serious fog.

Salesman with a product
I had to pump myself up to sell,
merchant of my own hope,
friend to every tollbooth man,
I named the trees I passed.
I knew the dwarf pines,
and why in such soil
they could grow only so tall.

A groundhog wobbled from the woods.
It, too, seemed ridiculous,
and I conjured for it a wild heart,
at least a wild heart.
My dashboard was agleam with numbers
and time.

It was the kind of morning
the dark never left.
The truly wild were curled up, asleep,
or in some high nest looking down.
There was no way they'd let us love them
just right.

I said "fine" to those who asked.
I told them about my sons, athletes both.
All day I moved among men
who claimed they needed nothing,
nothing, at least, that I had.
Maybe another time, they said,
or, Sorry, things are slow.

On the drive back
I drove fast, and met the regulars
at the Inn for a drink.
It seemed to me a man needed a heart
for the road, and a heart for home,
and one more for his friends.

And so many different, agile tongues.

JOY HARJO

The Path to the Milky Way Leads through Los Angeles

There are strangers above me, below me and all around me and we are all
strange in this place of recent invention.
This city named for angels appears naked and stripped of anything resembling
the shaking of turtle shells, the songs of human voices on a summer night
outside Okmulgee.
Yet, it's perpetually summer here, and beautiful. The shimmer of gods is easier
to perceive at sunrise or dusk,
when those who remember us here in the illusion of the marketplace

turn toward the changing of the sun and say our names.
We matter to somebody,
We must matter to the strange god who imagines us as we revolve together in
the dark sky on the path to the Milky Way.
We can't easily see that starry road from the perspective of the crossing of
boulevards, can't hear it in the whine of civilization or taste the minerals of
planets in hamburgers.
But we can buy a map here of the stars' homes, dial a tone for dangerous love,
choose from several brands of water or a hiss of oxygen for gentle
rejuvenation.
Everyone knows you can't buy love but you can still sell your soul for less
than a song to a stranger who will sell it to someone else for a profit
until you're owned by a company of strangers
in the city of the strange and getting stranger.
I'd rather understand how to sing from a crow
who was never good at singing or much of anything
but finding gold in the trash of humans.
So what are we doing here I ask the crow parading on the ledge of falling that
hangs over this precarious city?
Crow just laughs and says *wait, wait and see* and I am waiting and not seeing
anything, not just yet.
But like crow I collect the shine of anything beautiful I can find.

BILLY COLLINS

The Death of the Hat

Once every man wore a hat.

In the ashen newsreels,
the avenues of cities
are broad rivers flowing with hats.

The ballparks swelled
with thousands of straw hats,
brims and bands,

rows of men smoking
and cheering in shirtsleeves.

Hats were the law.
They went without saying.
You noticed a man without a hat in a crowd.

You bought them from Adams or Dobbs
who branded your initials in gold
on the inside band.

Trolleys crisscrossed the city.
Steamships sailed in and out of the harbor.
Men with hats gathered on the docks.

There was a person to block your hat
and a hatcheck girl to mind it
while you had a drink
or ate a steak with peas and a baked potato.
In your office stood a hat rack.

The day the war was declared
everyone in the street was wearing a hat
and they were wearing hats
when a ship loaded with men sank in the icy sea.

My father wore one to work every day
and returned home
carrying the evening paper,
the winter chill radiating from his overcoat.

But today we go bareheaded
into the winter streets,
stand hatless on frozen platforms.

Today the mailboxes on the roadside
and the spruce trees behind the house
wear cold white hats of snow.

Mice scurry from the stone walls at night
in their thin fur hats

to eat the birdseed that has spilled.

And now my father, after a life of work,
wears a hat of earth,
and on top of that,

A lighter one of cloud and sky—a hat of wind.

2000

In the garden, a large audience—very quiet &
perhaps listening—the light full but soft in the evening air,
air that one could breathe with pleasure.
—Philip Levine

Poems selected by Gray Jacobik
Fresh Voices poem selected by Mimi Madden

Featuring

Philip Levine

Marie Howe

Thomas Lux

Susan Kinsolving

Zach Sussman (Fresh Voices, Weston High School)

Martín Espada

Also read: Fresh Voices From Connecticut High Schools
Cailin Doyle, Miss Porters School
Andrew Drozd, Northwest Catholic High School
Stephanie Green, Newington High School
(also, Greater Hartford Academy of the Arts)
Scott Guild, Wethersfield High School
Erica Kim, E. O. Smith High School
Adrian Kudler, Hall High School
Sakima Stringer, E. O. Smith High School

Among Children

I walk among the rows of bowed heads —
the children are sleeping through fourth grade
so as to be ready for what is ahead,
the monumental boredom of junior high
and the rush forward tearing their wings
loose and turning their eyes forever inward.
These are the children of Flint, their fathers
work at the spark plug factory or truck
bottled water in 5 gallon sea-blue jugs
to the widows of the suburbs. You can see
already how their backs have thickened,
how their small hands, soiled by pig iron,
leap and stutter even in dreams. I would like
to sit down among them and read slowly
from *The Book of Job* until the windows
pale and the teacher rises out of a milky sea
of industrial scum, her gowns streaming
with light, her foolish words transformed
into song, I would like to arm each one
with a quiver of arrows so that they might
rush like wind there where no battle rages
shouting among the trumpets, Ha! Ha!
How dear the gift of laughter in the face
of the 8 hour day, the cold winter mornings
without coffee and oranges, the long lines
of mothers in old coats waiting silently
where the gates have closed. Ten years ago
I went among these same children, just born,
in the bright ward of the Sacred Heart and leaned
down to hear their breaths delivered that day,
burning with joy. There was such wonder
in their sleep, such purpose in their eyes
closed against autumn, in their damp heads

blurred with the hair of ponds, and not one
turned against me or the light, not one
said, I am sick, I am tired, I will go home,
not one complained or drifted alone,
unloved, on the hardest day of their lives.
Eleven years from now they will become
the men and women of Flint or Paradise,
the majors of a minor town, and I
will be gone into smoke or memory,
so I bow to them here and whisper
all I know, all I will never know.

MARIE HOWE

What the Living Do

Johnny, the kitchen sink has been clogged for days, some utensil probably
    fell down there.
And the Drano won't work but smells dangerous, and the crusty dishes
    have piled up

waiting for the plumber I still haven't called. This is the everyday we
    spoke of.
It's winter again: the sky's a deep headstrong blue, and the sunlight
    pours through

the open living room windows because the heat's on too high in here, and
    I can't turn it off.
For weeks now, driving, or dropping a bag of groceries in the street,
    the bag breaking,

I've been thinking: This is what the living do. And yesterday, hurrying
    along those
wobbly bricks in the Cambridge sidewalk, spilling my coffee down my
    wrist and sleeve,

I thought it again, and again later, when buying a hairbrush: This is it.
Parking. Slamming the car door shut in the cold. What you called
   that yearning.

What you finally gave up. We want the spring to come and the winter to
   pass. We want
whoever to call or not call, a letter, a kiss — we want more and more and
   then more of it.

But there are moments, walking, when I catch a glimpse of myself in the
   window glass,
say, the window of the corner video store, and I'm gripped by a cherishing
   so deep

for my own blowing hair, chapped face, and unbuttoned coat that I'm
   speechless:
I am living, I remember you.

THOMAS LUX

Refrigerator, 1957

More like a vault — you pull the handle out
and on the shelves: not a lot,
and what there is (a boiled potato
in a bag, a chicken carcass
under foil) looking dispirited,
drained, mugged. This is not
a place to go in hope or hunger.
But, just to the right of the middle
of the middle door shelf, on fire, a lit-from-within red,
heart red, sexual red, wet neon red,
shining red in the liquid, exotic,
aloof, slumming
in such company: a jar
of maraschino cherries. Three-quarters

full, fiery globes, like strippers
at a church social. Maraschino cherries, maraschino,
the only foreign word I knew. Not once
did I see these cherries employed: not
in a drink, nor on top
of a glob of ice cream,
or just pop one in your mouth. Not once.
The same jar there through an entire
childhood of dull dinners—bald meat,
pocked peas and, see above,
boiled potatoes. Maybe
they came over from the old country,
family heirlooms, or were status symbols
bought with a piece of the first paycheck
from a sweatshop,
which beat the pig farm in Bohemia,
handed down from my grandparents
to my parents
to be someday mine,
then my child's?
They were beautiful
and, if I never ate one,
it was because I knew it might be missed
or because I knew it would not be replaced
or because you do not eat
that which rips your heart with joy.

SUSAN KINSOLVING

My Late Father's Junk Mail

It arrives daily, promising insights
into the bond market, pest control
(free for the first month), getaway
vacations, subscriptions at discount,

coupons for vacuums, lubes, furnace
cleanings, and tire changes; specials
on cell phones and software. Some-
times, there's even a sample, a small

box of cereal, a single squeeze of tooth-
paste or shampoo. Charities of all sorts
want his donations, his pledge to help
cure disease, elect officials, advance

education, stop extinctions. Each crisis
needs him. And then they want his
opinion too! Surveys and sweepstakes
have his name in letters larger than life

urging him to hurry, rush, and not miss
out. Months ago, ocean waves enveloped
his ashes, but still these piles of paper
come, not even forwarded, just updated

as if he had moved in with me, his dutiful
daughter, who repeats his lambaste against
bureaucracy, advertising, and waste. I write
his rage. Here, postmortem is posthaste.

ZACH SUSSMAN

He Raises His Cup

The morning is warm
as a hound's underbelly.

Worn after a restless night,
my father drinks tea in the yard,
peculiar among crooked lilacs.

More & more he speaks of the future
as if it will not include him.

He raises his cup, wipes his brow.

I linger in the kitchen, bare feet
kissing cool tile, & watch the fine
beads of sweat collect below his chin.

It looks like his skin is crying.

MARTÍN ESPADA

Preciosa *Like a Last Cup of Coffee*

Tata says her wheelchair
has been stolen by the nurses.
She hallucinates the ceiling fan
spinning closer, the vertigo
of a plummeting helicopter,
but cannot raise her hands
against the blades. Her legs jerk
with the lightning that splits trees.
She scolds her dead sister,
who studies Tata's face
from a rocking chair by the bed
but does not answer.
The grandchildren are grateful
for the plastic diaper, the absence of bedsores.

Tata's mouth collapses without teeth;
her words are miners blackened in the hole.
Now a word pushes out: *café.*
No coffee for her, or she won't eat,
says the nurse.
Tata craves more than a puddle

in a styrofoam cup:
the coffee farm in Utuado, 1928,
the mountains hoisting a harvest of clouds,
the beans a handful of planets,
the spoon in the cup a silver oar,
and the roosters' bickering choir.

But no coffee today.
Cousin Bernice crawls into the bed,
stretches her body across Tata's body
like a drowsy lover, mouth hovering
before her grandmother's eyes
as she chants the word: *Preciosa.*

Preciosa like the song,
chorus brimming from a kitchen radio
on West 98th Street after the war,
splashing down the fire escape,
preciosa te llaman.
An island from the sky
or a last cup of coffee.
Tata repeats: *Preciosa.*
The song bathes her tongue.

2001

With Matisse inside the Hill-Stead, the largest audience I've read to in the garden, and music so lovely it blew me away, I remember thinking I was among marvelous things. And after the reading, I was covered in sweat.
—Edgar Gabriel Silex

Poems selected by Patricia Hale
Fresh Voices poem selected by Mimi Madden

Featuring

Sonia Sanchez

Rennie McQuilkin

Linda McCarriston

Edgar Gabriel Silex

Emily Madsen (Fresh Voices, Avon High School)

Peter Schmitt (winner, 10th anniversary Sunken Garden poetry contest)

Doug Anderson

Also read: Fresh Voices from Connecticut High Schools

Maggie Crowley, Miss Porter's School

Tarray Daniels, South Windsor High School

(also, Greater Hartford Academy of the Arts)

Cassandra Faustini, Bunnell High School

Chris Gyngell, E. O. Smith High School

Rebekah Hayes, Suffield High School

(also, Greater Hartford Academy of the Arts)

Amy Ma, Conard High School

Ballad

(after the Spanish)

forgive me if i laugh
you are so sure of love
you are so young
and i too old to learn of love.

the rain exploding
in the air is love
the grass excreting her
green wax is love
and stones remembering
past steps is love,
but you. you are too young
for love
and i too old.

once, what does it matter
when or who, i knew
of love.
i fixed my body
under his and went
to sleep in love
all trace of me
was wiped away

forgive me if i smile
young heiress of a naked dream
you are so young
and i too old to learn of love.

We All Fall Down

for Kelly, my student

Her turn had come. She knew
by heart almost
the lines she was to speak
but gave us, God help her,

the truth
beyond the lines,
beyond the book she dropped,
its pages thrashing to the floor
like broken wings—

the truth
she beat her head upon,
bit into so hard
I could not pry her jaws,
teeth grinding—

the truth beyond us
she saw as ever,
her risen eyes gone white
as bone.

I did what I could,
I held her and held her, seized
with sudden love and knowing
we all fall down.

In the end
I carried her curled in my arms
across one threshold
and another.

Birthday Girl: 1950

for my mother

The day the package came
from Sears, you were ironing
and smoking, in the one
slab of light that elbowed in
between our three-decker
and the next one.
World Series Time, and the radio
bobbing on the square end
of the board told over
what you already knew:

The Sox are the same old
bunch of bums! you said, slamming
the iron into some navy gabardine;
the smells of workclothes — Tide
and oil — rose up together
in steam around you, like the roar
of the crowd at Fenway
and the shouts, downstairs,
of Imalda, getting belted around
her kitchen at noon.

Some people can make anything
out of anything else. If you
still can, remember that day
like this: you douse your cigarette
and squat down close; I open
the box addressed only to me
and find inside the pair of sandals
you call harlequin, with straps
as many colored as a life.

I am happy. You buckle them on me.
Every room is dark but where we are.
Every other room is empty.

EDGAR GABRIEL SILEX

Distances

for Sherman Alexie

as a child I thought my grandfather was a god
who walked out each dawn and pulled the sun up
by the songstrings of birds who sang to his presence
I thought being old meant it was easier
to finally take for granted each last dawn
yet there he was each morning going out
offering himself to the momentary
to the spiraling motion that it would continue on
to the sun so that it would continue to rise
like incense he would rise in the rose-light
of his thank yous *thank you weaver of this*
green-blue earth thank you maker of this
blue-green sky for my wife for my family
for this morning when we sat together
at the breakfast table his thank yous
would smile us awake I think now

that she was god's hand turning the machinery
of the day the washing thrashing and hanging
of our clothes the cutting stirring and pouring
the nursing of hungers and pains shushing
and brushing our childhood vims my grandmother turning
everything slowly till it hummed into each
night's silence like that corner of hers
where she kept a candle and cross in the quiet
of her bedroom where she rooted her knees

her hands clasped and heavy as the bags
of her eyes her whispers rising evanescing
in the stillness *God keep my good husband sober*
and strong please don't make us choose
between food and the mortgage please forgive
our transgressions in the darkness she kissed
Amens softly on our sleeping foreheads

a Spanish Catholic she preferred to speak
of herself simply by saying she was Castillian
a full Indian he preferred to say nothing
in that way he spoke of how all our blood is
indivisible but once when I was little she cried
as she tried to whip the stubborn Indian
out of us he always dreamed about
what might happen she always dreamed
of what had happened and I am amazed
at how they loved each other
at how this world marries the impossible
at how each night and day they taught us
to think good thankful thoughts but mostly
I am in awe at how the word *please*
eventually frees the soul it tries
to destroy with its slavery

EMILY MADSEN

Listening to My Father Practice

When my father holds his guitar
it is a large and fragile yellow bird
with shiny plumage and a single black eye.

He strokes its feathers and it sings

Sometimes,
the guitar's giant unblinking eye
captures the emotions of all that came before.
Passive observer,
it hides them all away in its deep wooden belly,
where the sides slope like immense ribs, slow and round

There they perch,
like sparrows in the eaves of a tired old barn,
until my father puts his fingers
to the strings with his singular thoughts,
and the sparrows drop from the cavernous darkness
and spread their wings,
each speaking their particular name.

But tonight the birds are in my father's heart,
and when his gentle hands hold the guitar
it becomes the channel from his ribcage
to the sky.

PETER SCHMITT

Packing Plant

They must have thought I was spying on them,
my father's employees in the packing plant—
me, the boss's kid, scribbling during breaks
inside the latticed cab of a forklift.
How could I tell them those notes were poetry?

I could barely convince myself. But still
I filled the pages of the little pad,
while the place roared around me: trucks backing in,
dirt from the fields still caked in their treads; washes
and steam, groan of conveyor belts; the shouts,

the clatter of cans rattling down a chute,
hiss of boilers, and all of it echoing—
but whatever I found the concentration
to write about, it was never the plant
or its people: not the ladies on the line

in their yellow rubber boots and gloves, hairnets,
pulling, like editors, each tomato
gone soft or black or too small, shifting their weight
when their hips then knees then backs began to ache;
not Willie Cunningham, who steered a forklift

with one long black finger, who could whirl it
on a Liberty dime he'd been at it
so long, while I couldn't even drive a car
yet, banging the forks against the pallets;
Willie, who in a couple of years would lose

his testicles to cancer, my father
visiting him in the hospital, as I
waited in the car. None of it seemed worth
writing about, not even my own job,
trundling the emptied produce bins to storage,

building them to the rafters forty feet high—
not that, or the way the lunchtime whistle
would carry like a train's, shaking the beams
of the little whitewashed churches down the road,
and bring the workers forward from the dark—

and maybe I really *was* spying on them,
and just didn't know it: too busy stacking
stanzas like bins all the way to the sky—
until the next truck rumbled in with its load
and I shifted, awkwardly, into gear.

Blues

Love won't behave. I've tried
all my life to keep it chained up.
Especially after I gave up pleading.
I don't mean the woman,
but the love itself. Truth is,
I don't know where it comes from,
why it comes, or where it goes.
It either leaves me feeling the knife
of my first breath
or hang-dog and sick
at someone else's unstoppable
and as the blues song says,
can't sit down, stand up, lay down pain.
Right now I want it.
I'm like a country who can't remember the last war.
Well, that's not strictly true.
It's just been too long.
Too long and my heart is like
a house for sale in a lot full of high weeds.
I want to go down to New Orleans
and find the Santeria woman
who will light a whole table full of candles
and moan things, place a cigar
and a shot of whiskey in front of Chango's picture
and kiss the blue dead Jesus on the wall.
I want something.
Used to be I'd get a bottle
and drink until the lights went out
but now I carry my pain around everywhere I go
because I'm afraid
I might put it down somewhere and lose it.
I've grown tender about my mileage.

My teeth are like Stonehenge and my tongue
is like an old druid fallen in a ditch.
A soul is like a shrimper's net they never haul up
and it's full of everything:
A tire. A shark. An old harpoon.
A kid's plastic bucket.
An empty half-pint.
A broken guitar string.
A pair of ballerina's shoes with the ribbons tangled
in an anchor chain.
And the net gets heavier until the boat
starts to go down with it and you say,
God, what is going on.
In this condition I say love is a good thing.
I'm ready to capsize.
I can't even see the shoreline.
I haven't seen a seagull in three days.
I'm ready to drink salt water,
go overboard and start swimming.
Suffice it to say I want to get in the bathtub
with the Santeria woman and steam myself pure again.
The priest that blesses the water may be bored.
Hung over. He may not even bless it,
just tell people he did. It doesn't matter.
What the Santeria woman puts on it with her mind
makes it like a holy mirror.
You can float a shrimp boat on it.
The spark that jumps between her mind
and the priest's empty act
is what makes the whole thing light up
like an oilslick on fire against a sunset over Oaxaca.
So if I just step out into it.
If I just step off the high dive over a pool
that may or may not have water in it;
that act is enough
to connect the two poles of something
and make a long blue arc.

I don't have a clue about any of this.
Come on over here and love me.
I used to say that drunk.
Now I am stark raving sober
and I say, Come on over here and love me.

2002

Whole families unfold their lawn chairs and settle in, as if they have come not for poems but for fireworks, staying until well past twilight. And there you are, setting off rockets and high twizzlers, often to murmurs of pleasure and applause. We're doing it all wrong, America! Poets belong outdoors in the grass among the trees, and their poetry belongs to the people!
—Wesley McNair

Poems selected by Brad Davis
Fresh Voices poem selected by Mimi Madden

Featuring

Yusef Komunyakaa

Vivian Shipley

Wesley McNair

Marilyn Chin

Jennifer Steele (Fresh Voices, Middletown High School)

Steve Straight

Also read: Fresh Voices from Connecticut High Schools
Catherine Adams-Besancon, Watkinson School
Yiyin Erin Chen, Simsbury High School
Hannah Goldfield, Wilbur Cross High School
Johanna Klotz, Newington High School
(also, Greater Hartford Academy of the Arts)
Laurel Mandelberg, Simsbury High School
Cindy Martinez, A. I. Prince Technical High School
(also, Greater Hartford Academy of the Arts)

Facing It

My black face fades,
hiding inside the black granite.
I said I wouldn't,
dammit: No tears.
I'm stone. I'm flesh.
My clouded reflection eyes me
like a bird of prey, the profile of night
slanted against morning. I turn
this way—the stone lets me go.
I turn that way—I'm inside
the Vietnam Veterans Memorial
again, depending on the light
to make a difference.
I go down the 58,022 names,
half-expecting to find
my own in letters like smoke.
I touch the name Andrew Johnson;
I see the booby trap's white flash.
Names shimmer on a woman's blouse
but when she walks away
the names stay on the wall.
Brushstrokes flash, a red bird's
wings cutting across my stare.
The sky. A plane in the sky.
A white vet's image floats
closer to me, then his pale eyes
look through mine. I'm a window.
He's lost his right arm
inside the stone. In the black mirror
a woman's trying to erase names:
No, she's brushing a boy's hair.

Martha Stewart's Ten Commandments for Snow

   I. Make the paths neat with a slight curve. Leave at
least an inch of snow. Aesthetics are important.

  II. Pack perpendicular walls of snow. Cross country
ski through them to the gym. Snowshoe to work.

 III. Walk your dog. Always hang a little whisk broom
on your wrist. When you see yellow snow, remove it.

 IV. If you are old, stay in your own home if you have one.
Tie grosgrain ribbons on sheets. Wash the gold china.

  V. It takes two hours to make a snow cave. If you don't
hibernate balled in like a snake, an igloo takes three.

 VI. You can sleep out at five below zero. It will be cozy.
Dream a little. Dye the iced walls with food coloring.

VII. Wrap yourself in layers of pastel tissue from Chanel.
If you are poor, newspaper, cardboard, just anything.

VIII. Hypothermia could set in. First signs are that you feel
weak or sleepy. Keep someone nearby, a bottle will do.

 IX. The body is a furnace. Funnel or pour anything handy
into your mouth — 86 calories per hour or 2,000 a day.

  X. You may have problems walking on ice and fall down.
Don't beg. In calligraphy, letter: Please Pick Me Up.

The One I Think of Now

At the end of my stepfather's life
when his anger was gone,
and the saplings of his failed
nursery had grown into trees,
my newly feminist mother had him
in the kitchen to pay for all
those years he only did the carving.
"You know where that is,"
she would say as he looked
for a knife to cut the cheese
and a tray to serve it with,
his apron wide as a dress
above his work boots, confused
as a girl. He is the one I think of now,
lifting the tray for my family,
the guests, until at last he comes
to me. And I, no less confused,
look down from his hurt eyes as if
there were nothing between us
except an arrangement of cheese,
and not this bafflement, these
almost tender hands that once
swung hammers and drove machines
and insisted that I learn to be a man.

25 Haiku

A hundred red fire ants scouring, scouring the white peony

Fallen plum blossoms return to the branch, you sleep, then harden again

Cuttlefish in my palm stiffens with rigor mortis, boy toys can't love

Neighbor's barn: grass mat, crickets, Blue Boy, trowel handle, dress soaked in mud

Iron-headed mace; double-studded halberd slice into emptiness

O fierce Oghuz, tie me to two wild elephants, tear me in half

O my swarthy herder, two-humped bactrian, drive me the long distance

Forceps, tongs, *bushi*, whip, flanks, scabbard, stirrup, goads, distaff, wither, awl

Black-eyed Susans, Queen Anne's lace, bounty of cyclamen, mown paths erupt

Gaze at the charred hills, the woe-be-gone kiosks, we are all God's hussies

I have not fondled the emperor's lap dog, whose name is Black Muzzle

Urge your horses into the mist-swilled Galilee, O sweet Bedlamite

Her Majesty's randying up the jewel stairs to find the pleasure dome

Ancient pond; the frog jumps in and in and in: the deep slap of water

The frog jumps into the ancient pond; she says, no, I am not ready

Coyote cooked his dead wife's vagina and fed it to his new wife

I plucked out three white pubic hairs and they turned into flying monkeys

Let's do it on the antimacassar, on the antimacassar.

Little Red drew her teeny pistol from her basket and said "eat me"

Sing sing little yellow blight rage rage against the dying of the light

Chimera: Madame Pol Pot grafting a date tree onto a date tree

His unworthy appendage, his mutinous henchman grazed my pink cheeks

He on top now changes to bottom, Goddess welcomes her devotee

Fish fish fowl fowl, mock me Mistress Bean-curd, I am both duck and essence

Don't touch him, bitch, we're engaged; and besides, he's wearing my nipple-ring

---

JENNIFER STEELE

To Be the Lighter Shade of Black

I wasn't born dark skinned,
Milk Chocolate,
Or even honey brown.
God didn't make me in the image
Of a voluptuous backside
Or thick waist.
No.
He created me daffodil yellow,
Slim,
And thin lipped.

Right now you're wondering
What does this mean
While
All my life I've asked myself,
"Where
do I belong?"

At Spike's Garage

At Spike's Garage near the university
I pull in for gas. It's the olden days,
and Ernie the mechanic comes out
from the bay to pump my gas.

I'm in grad school and my second year
teaching freshman English, and Ernie's
fixed my car a few times at his house
to spare me Spike's cut for parts and labor.

Ernie, a townie, about 22, bushy haired
with greasy blue coveralls, oil under
his nails, locks the pump on and says,
"So, professor, what're ya teachin'?"

It's Friday, and I remember the dazed group
I tried to teach that morning, sleepy and
hung over, leading a discussion one more
session pulling teeth. "Hamlet,"
I tell him. "You know, Shakespeare."

He stops in mid-squeegee as blue water
streams down my window. "Hamlet!"
he spits. "Ugh. I had to read that in
high school. It was awful, so boring."

He seems to say what my students only
thought, and for a second I wonder if
I'm cut out for this, trying to teach great
works to people who hate them.

"Hamlet!" he says again, shaking
the squeegee. "He didn't even know
when to shit." Finally he pulls it across
the window, wiping the excess liquid off
the rubber with his fingers. "Macbeth,"
he says. "Now *that* was a play."

2003

*A steady rain drove us into the local Congregational
church. The audience was warm and supportive
as I stood nervously in the undeserved pulpit.*
— *Maxine Kumin*

Poems selected by Sue Ellen Thompson
Fresh Voices poem selected by Mimi Madden

Featuring

Maxine Kumin

Jack Agüeros

Margaret Gibson

Tim Seibles

Hailey Gallant (Fresh Voices: E. O. Smith High School)

Tony Fusco (winner, Sunken Garden Poetry Prize)

Wally Swist

Also read: Fresh Voices from Connecticut High Schools
Ashley Coleman, Thomas Snell Weaver High School
(also, Greater Hartford Academy of the Arts
Laura Marris, Hopkins School
Sarah Mikolowsky, RHAM High School
Sarah Myers, E. O. Smith High School
Emily Paige Steinert, Enfield Adult Education Diploma Program

Morning Swim

Into my empty head there come
a cotton beach, a dock wherefrom

I set out, oily and nude
through mist, in chilly solitude.

There was no line, no roof or floor
to tell the water from the air.

Night fog thick as terry cloth
closed me in its fuzzy growth.

I hung my bathrobe on two pegs.
I took the lake between my legs.

Invaded and invader, I
went overhand on that flat sky.

Fish twitched beneath me, quick and tame.
In their green zone they sang my name

and in the rhythm of the swim
I hummed a two-four-time slow hymn.

I hummed "Abide With Me." The beat
rose in the fine thrash of my feet,

rose in the bubbles I put out
slantwise, trailing through my mouth.

My bones drank water; water fell
through all my doors. I was the well

that fed the lake that met my sea
in which I sang "Abide With Me."

Psalm for Distribution

Lord,
on 8th Street
between 6th Avenue and Broadway
there are enough shoe stores
with enough shoes
to make me wonder
why there are shoeless people
on the earth.

Lord,
You have to fire the Angel
in charge of distribution.

Strange Altars

> *Who sends the mind to wander far?*
> *Who first drives life to start on its journey?*
> *Who impels us to utter these words?*
> *Who is the Spirit behind the eye and the ear?*

To steady my heart I say these words, to keep me
    each morning
before the altar in my study, a footstool

    on which I have placed
the head of the Buddha, the gilt rubbed off,
    one lowered eyelid worn gold.

Fixed to a spike, the head of the Buddha's
      fit to a small wood block
for balance, not for permanence — the body of the Buddha

      gone its own way, the head
changed from temple plunder to exotic fragment,
      a bit of inscrutable ruin.

The topknot of flame, the *Ushnisha*, geysers up
      like a gothic spire
from the skullcap of close corkscrew curls.

      Ears pendulous, nostrils
flared, eyebrows the wings of a seabird
      afloat on a thermal. And the mouth,

I love the mouth, how it's puckered in the loose
      serenity of a smile that lingers
when one's been kissed, the lover no longer

      there in the room.
And so I sit, *certain of nothing* — some mornings
      not even that.

Who sends the mind to wander far — who brings it
      home? You think
this asking is easy? A rationed calm? An abeyance,

      flowing and cool?
Eat the question, you swallow fire — a ruthless
      unoathed fire that

swallows you completely. Exactly what I want,
      the head of the Buddha
rests on the white rebozo I bought in Oaxaca —

rests on a remembered
aroma of sweat and dust and dried herbs in a basket,
        ropes of *chile de arbol*

red as the shriek of the small pig hoisted behind
        a bright blind
of zinnias and callas, its throat about to be cut.

TIM SEIBLES

Natasha in a Mellow Mood

    (apologies to Bullwinkle & Rocky)

Boris, dahlink, look
at my legs, long
as a lonely evening in Leningrad,
how they open the air
when I walk, the way moonlight
opens the dark. Boris, my hair

is so black with espionage,
so cool and quiet with all those secrets
so well kept—those secret plans
you've nearly kissed
into my ears. Who gives a proletarian
damn about Bullwinkle and that
flying squirrel and that idiot
who draws us? America

is a virgin, the cartoonist who leaves me
less than a Barbie doll under
this dress, who draws me
with no smell—he is a virgin.
The children who watch us
every Saturday mornink
are virgins. Boris, my sweet waterbug, I

don't want to be a virgin anymore.
Look into my eyes, heavy with
the absence of laughter
and the presence of vodka. Listen
to my Russian lips muss up
these blonde syllables of English:

Iwantchu. Last night
I dreamed you spelled your
code name on my shoulder
with the waxed sprigs of your
moustache. I had just come
out of the bath. My skin was still

damp, my hair poured like ink
as I pulled the comb through it. Then
I heard you whisper, felt you take
my hand—Oh, Boris, Boris
Badenov, I want your mischief-
riddled eyes to invent

my whole body, all the silken
slopes of flesh forgotten
by the blind cartoonist. I want
to be scribbled all over you
in shapes no pencil would dare. Dahlink,

why don't we take off
that funny little hat. Though
you are hardly tall
as my thighs, I want your pointy
shoes beside my bed, your
coat flung and fallen
like a double-agent
on my floor.

Roots

I come from a long line
of Portuguese women.
Venho de una lina longa
de mulheres Portuguese.
From women,
que nao falm Portuguese
but still hold it high
above their heads
like banners.
Eu origino de una Ava
who raised her 5 boys
(and her one *menia*)
the best she could.
Alone
because her husband
turned *alcoolico.*
E de sua mae
who left her country,
alone
with a baby girl
in her belly
because her husband
was too poor to afford
two tickets
to *os Estados Unidos.*
And now, my Irish side
asks why I think I
am made of steel.
My lungs ask my heart why
I'm so stubborn
"too independent."
Why I get along
so well

alone.
And my eyes answer
as the first in many generations —
Em Portuguese.
"I come from a long line
of *mulheres*
Portugeses fortes."
And I wave it
above my head
like a banner.

TONY FUSCO

The Litany of Streets

Catching some lights we roll down Howard Avenue,
pass Rosette. My father tells me this was once a nice
part of town. He does not drive, has never driven a car,

his geography limited to the bus routes, and how far
he could walk. He has been a prolific walker. As we turn
onto Columbus Avenue he says: *See the dome on that church?*

It used to be all gold. I've heard it all before. *Gold leaf
it was beautiful — St. Anthony's. San Antonio, pray for us.*
I correct him, pointing out the church is Sacred Heart.

St. Anthony's is the building less than a block away.
Sacred Heart? he asks. *Once, all these streets used to run
down to the railroad, trolleys one way, and a block over
you could catch another going the other way.* I would say

something, but he starts again. *Pop worked on the railroad.
His brother and uncle John, they were all railroad men.*
On South Frontage Road he says what he misses the most

is the flea market. *You could go around on a Saturday
and there would always be something valuable to find,
always something good. Everything was old there, but there*

was always something new to you. He stops. *That's the
Prince Street School, I went to school there.* I've heard this
before as well, heard it all before. The building is refinished,

its red brick bright in the sunlight, it is now a medical building.
To the right, the old Lee High School sits on top of half of what
once was Liberty Street. It is where the house he grew up in

stood, before the highway came through, before redevelopment.
I ask anyway. Isn't that where you were born? *No.* His answer
Is a surprise, something new on a Saturday. *I asked my mother*

*one day, Ma, which hospital was I born in? And she says, you
weren't born in a hospital, you were born on Lafayette Street.*
After fifty years and all the talk of neighborhoods and houses,

of stores and movie theaters, I had thought he had only
lived in that one house he always talked about. I've written
down a family history. Here is something once lost, forgotten.

We are both quiet, the litany of streets has stopped. We turn
onto Church, wordless past Chapel, to Elm, to Olive
to Lucibello's bakery. He is retired, still all the employees

love him. My father, last of the old timer bakers left since
Frank died. *Hey Tony! Take some zeppoles.* Johnny fills
the white cardboard box, tying it with red stripe string.

*Come in again. Don't be a stranger. We miss you. Nobody
knows anything anymore, how to make the cream, how to paint
the cookies.* He beams. Back in the car I turn down Grand Avenue

determined to go home by another route. *You know,* my father
says, *I had an aunt who had a house here on James Street.*
I listen carefully, against the day when memories fail.

Guardian Angel

after Rolf Jacobsen

For years I have been trying to find the patience
to listen to the resonant whisper of her voice
tickling my ear. Sometimes I imagine I see her,

the one who keeps me calm, whose guiding hands
steer me out of the shallows of my own making;
who walks on a cool, dustless path; who presses

her head against my heart, whose arms around
my shoulders lift by morning; who awakens in me
a vision of the ruby in the hummingbird's song.

2004

*As we stood at the top of the stone steps, and I saw the
beautiful garden, I thought to myself, "Wow. I can't wait to see
this evening's program!" And a second later I realized — for
the first time? — that it was I who was on the program.*
— *Suzanne Cleary*

Poems selected by Steve Straight
Fresh Voices poem selected by Mimi Madden

Featuring

Grace Paley

Richard Blanco

Suzanne Cleary (winner, Sunken Garden Poetry Prize)

Joan Joffe Hall

Martha Collins

Emily Ayer (Fresh Voices, Ledyard High School)

Kate Rushin

Also read: Fresh Voices from Connecticut High Schools
Stephen Frechette, Westminster School
Hannah Katch, Sudbury Valley Democratic School (East Woodstock resident)
Nicole Oliva, RHAM High School
Eric Serrano, Wilby High School
Jaclyn Sheltry, Ledyard High School

Here

Here I am in the garden laughing
an old woman with heavy breasts
and a nicely mapped face

how did this happen
well that's who I wanted to be

at last a woman
in the old style sitting
stout thighs apart under
a big skirt grandchild sliding
on off my lap a pleasant
summer perspiration

that's my old man across the yard
he's talking to the meter reader
he's telling him the world's sad story
how electricity is oil or uranium
and so forth I tell my grandson
run over to your grandpa ask him
to sit beside me for a minute I
am suddenly exhausted by my desire
to kiss his sweet explaining lips.

Winter of the Volcanoes: Guatemala

Because rain clouds shade the valley all summer,
they call this their winter, and I'm here, witness
to the rains of August, surrounded by volcanoes.

Volcanoes everywhere, like cathedrals at the end
of every stretch of cobblestone I wobble through.
Volcanoes, triangulating the view in every window,
reading over my shoulders on the terrace at night,
funneling stars between their peaks, threatening
to grumble and leave *la Antigua* to rise a third time
out of ruin. Volcanoes, keeping watch like a council
of four unforgiving gods: Acatenango, Fuego, Agua,
and Pacaya — the one I climbed, step by step through
rows of corn groomed like manes by Mayan hands,
through the quilt work of terrace farmers' patches,
through clouds veiling through pinewood forests,
until I walked in pumice fields, barren as the moon,
if the moon were black, spelled out my name with
freshly minted stones I laid down to claim *I was here*
on this newly kilned rock that in a few eons will be
the soil of the valley, the earth I savor in my coffee,
the dust settling over window sills and counter tops.
I scaled the peak, reached the crater's lip, stood silent
over the cauldron of molten, blood-orange petals,
the pearlescent fire, an open wound weeping smoke,
terrified I might fall, terrified that, for a moment,
I'd let myself be seduced by the pure, living heart
of the raw earth, saying: *here, let me take you back.*

SUZANNE CLEARY

Anyways

> *for David*

Anyone born anywhere near
    my home town says it this way,
        with an *s* on the end:
            "The lake is cold but I swim in it anyways,"
            "Kielbasa gives me heartburn but I eat it anyways,"

"(She/he) treats me bad, but I love (her/him) anyways."
Even after we have left that place
        and long settled elsewhere, this
                is how we say it, plural.
                        I never once, not once, thought twice about it
                until my husband, a man from far away,
        leaned toward me, one day during our courtship,
his grey-green eyes, which always sparkle,
        doubly sparkling over our candle-lit meal.
                "Anyway," he said. And when he saw
                        that I didn't understand, he repeated the word:
                "Anyway. *Way*, not *ways*."
        Corner of napkin to corner of lip, he waited.
I kept him waiting. I knew he was right,
        but I kept him waiting anyways,
                in league, still, with me and mine:
                        Slovaks homesick for the Old Country their whole lives
                who dug gardens anyways,
        and deep, hard-water wells.
I looked into his eyes, their smoky constellations,
        and then I told him. It is *anyways*, plural,
                because the word must be large enough
        to hold all of our reasons. *Anyways* is our way
of saying there is more than one reason,
        and there is that which is beyond reason,
                that which cannot be said.
                        A man dies and his widow keeps his shirts.
                They are big but she wears them anyways.
The shoemaker loses his life savings in the Great Depression
but gets out of bed, every day, anyways.
        We are shy, my people, not given to storytelling.
                We end our stories too soon, trailing off "Anyways . . ."
                        The carpenter sighs, "I didn't need that finger anyways."
                The beauty school student sighs, "It'll grow back anyways."
        Our faith is weak, but we go to church anyways.
The priest at St. Cyril's says God loves us. We hear what isn't said.
        This is what he must know about me, this man, my love.
                My people live in the third rainiest city in the country,

but we pack our picnic baskets as the sky darkens.
We fall in love knowing it may not last, but we fall.
This is how we know *home*:
someone who will look into our eyes
and say what could ruin everything, but say it,
regardless.

JOAN JOFFE HALL

Seed Sack

A child uprooted us from bed, had breakfast
ready, sausage, eggs and toast. We were proud
in this dream. I dreamed that babies were exposed
in birds' nests *in the tree top*, or fell from ladders,
or stepped with abandon into the road.
Sad, *dead*, even *proud*—I hear the thud
of the final "D" as the past gallops off.

I dreamed we'd built a barn
for storing all our stuff. Locking up
after a barn-warming I carried a twenty-pound
sack of seeds inside and turned to snap
the back door shut. The bag grabbed hold,
its corners sprouted arms and legs. "This bag
is holding on to me like a baby," I told
you. A baby past first infancy
and knowing how to grip. The sack kept
growing, became a two-year-old.
But still I knew it was just a burlap bag
I'd have to leave behind. And yet I couldn't
quite say to it: *But you're only a seed sack!*
It whined and wanted toys to play with
and I found some bolts and screws I hoped
would please it and laid it gently, sadly,
on a bed. I was torn but had to go.

In my waking life, a little Chinese girl,
abandoned when she was two days old,
has been adopted by a friend of ours.
How do you say to such a child —
I can hardly write the words without
evoking the shudder of the dream —
Someone threw you away, but I wanted you.

MARTHA COLLINS

Field

The window fell out the window
and having only a frame
to refer to, we entered

a new field, the space filled
with lightness, wheat field, sweet
field, field of vision, field

and ground, and the puzzle became
the principle, a page without
a single tree, but you kept coming

back to the place, your fingers
reading my skin, and I cried Love!
before I could stop myself, love

is a yellow shirt, light
is what it thinks when it thinks
of itself, and now it shines

through both our skins, in
the field, out of the field,
two in the field where none

had been, field to field
with particles stirred
into being where we touch.

EMILY AYER

Sacrilege

When I was young, I regretted that my religion
didn't call for crossing oneself.
I mourned the absence of Catholic aerobics,
especially of kneeling—
not on a small rug,
not even on an upholstered rail,
though I imagined that the stiff brocade
might press small designs into my flesh.
This I wouldn't mind,
I thought, as I envisioned tracing with one finger
the angelic tattoo embroidered on my skin.

I lamented the lack of
slender sticks smoldering in a silver dish,
loosing a sticky sweet scent,
and I longed for bitter and tangy leaves,
crushed into a box swung by the Papal hand.
I wanted to faint
from the heady aroma, yet
all I received was a wafer-thin paper bulletin,
pressed into my small hand every Sunday,
smelling faintly of the
church secretary's perfume—
a musty mix of Chanel No. 5 and
baby powder.

Going to Canada

In Quebec, Canada, Mommy and I climb up to
St. Anne De Bow—pray on our knees
praying the prayer on the sign on each step.
The altar is a mountain of braces and crutches
thrown away by the healed people.

Daddy lets us stop at the restaurant.
I ask Mommy if they have French food.
Green cheese? The waitress asks.
Green cheese?

The big hotel room is all fringes,
patterns, textures, carved tables and chairs.
I think Europe must be like this.
The chambermaid picks up my Tiny Tears doll.
She wears a uniform like in the movies
and asks me questions in French.
I understand exactly what she is saying, but
I'm not sure how to answer.
I look at my mother who smiles and says go on . . .

On our way out of town Dad stops for gas—
one giant, squeaky balloon, free, with a fill-up.
Mommy, can you tell me what to say:
Uh-baa-luh-see-vou-play.
The balloon shrivels before the next bathroom stop.
Uh-baa-luh-see-vou-play.

2005

As dusk fell, and individual faces grew indistinct,
then faded into the darkness, it seemed then as if I was
reading poetry in a shared dream.
— *Cortney Davis*

Poems selected by Margaret Gibson
Fresh Voices poem selected by Mimi Madden

Featuring

Gary Soto

Edwina Trentham

Douglas Goetsch (runner-up, Sunken Garden Poetry Prize)

Brad Davis (winner, Sunken Garden Poetry Prize)

Major Jackson

Lily Press (Fresh Voices, Danbury High School)

Cortney Davis

Also read: Fresh Voices from Connecticut High Schools
Jessica Kim, Wethersfield High School
(also, Greater Hartford Academy of the Arts)
Lisa Kim, Simsbury High School
Molly LaFlesh, Rockville High School
Tonya Malinowski, Newington High School
(also, Greater Hartford Academy of the Arts)
Maya Polan, Wilbur Cross High School (also, Educational Center for the Arts)

The Skeptics

Pyrrho of Elis and Sextus Empiricus were Skeptics,
Two big-shot thinkers who argued
Over figs, wine, and the loveliness of their sex.
I crowed to my brother about them,
And one evening
With Fig Newton crumbs around our mouths,
I was Pyrrho and Rick was Sextus,
Both of us skeptical about getting good jobs.
I said, "Brother Sextus,
What will you render on the canvas
When you're all grown up?" He chewed
His Fig Newton and answered, "Pyrrho,
My young flame, I will draw the reality
Of dead dogs with their feet in the air."
I crowed, "Wow, Rick — I mean Sextus — that's awesome!"
In sandals, we went to the liquor store,
Each of us in our imaginary robes,
And stole a quart of beer. Neither of us
Was skeptic when we swigged on that quart
And walked past the house
Where a woman hammered on walnuts,
The rise and fall of her buttery hand quivering
The two hairs on my chest. We had figs and wine,
And what we Skeptics needed
Were three strokes of that hammering.
I flowed over in my robe
And said, "We're Brother Skeptics,
Ruled by cautious truths." She smiled,
Hammer raised, and said, "Sure you are."
Right away we got along, a womanly skeptic
With a nice swing. I sat on the steps,
A young man with his figs, his wine,
And, with my Greek named shed,
Reverent believer in a woman with hammer in hand.

My Father's Gift

Hearing of my failure,
my father turned his face
from death for the moment,
and we spent my sixteenth
summer enclosed in screen
and limestone, a porch
high above the harbor,
where he taught me to take
apart those solid blocks
of Latin that scholars love
to call "the unseen." Head
bent to the book, long fingers
resting on the uneasy
card-table, he returned

to his Oxford days, the blithe,
young scholar fifty years gone
by then, handed me the keys
to those blank walls of words,
and we passed through them
together. And so, as the sun
skipped coins of light
on the sea below, and oleander
drifted pink and white
in the corner of my eye,
I learned to love the unseen.

I have lost all my Latin
now, but this morning,
when I opened his Christ
Church notebook, I found
again what he gave me
that summer — set down

in cramped filigree, thirty
years and more before
my birth, the life
of the mind, exuberant,
contained, still blossoming
on the faded page.

DOUGLAS GOETSCH

Sofa-Bed

My last girlfriend broke my bed. Yes
we were having sex on it, and maybe
you think I was at least half responsible,
but she was the one who liked to drift
up into the corner of the padded back
where she'd spread her arms like a queen,
and all I could think of was the man
who sold me this fifteen-hundred dollar
sofa-bed, warning me never to put
extra weight where the head should be,
which was exactly where our bodies were,
humping the morning, she in her
careless abandon, me unable to get
the octagonal rims of the salesman's glasses
out of my head; she producing
lovely, husky groans, me listening
to the complaining of springs and joints
and hollow chrome. She would have
scolded me for such a concern —
a piece of furniture compared to living
in the moment, the pleasure of a woman,
a woman who was, after all this time,
adjusting me to intimacy, wanting me
to connect and come, though I didn't
see why this all couldn't take place

a few feet down and to the left.
Soon it wasn't happening at all,
and in the end I found I could tell
her everything except this—better
to have her think my head was full
of other women, or baseball, than discover
I was Felix Ungar guarding the coffee table,
ready with a coaster to ruin his life.
She left me with a convex bed. I sleep
as though on a boulder, feet and head
lower than my chest, listening to the traffic
on Greenwich Avenue, which never stops.

BRAD DAVIS

Common as Air

When Mrs. Weiss told us in earth science,
a light, limb-filtered breeze blessing us
through the room's west wall windows,
that somewhere camouflaged within
our every lung-full of air marches air

Hitler breathed and Khrushchev and
Richard Speck, I began breathing less—
shorter intakes, pauses after each exhale—
willing to endure panicky bursts of craving
in exchange for reducing the likelihood

of those radioactive atoms passing
from lung to blood to brain. If she included
mention of the Buddha or Madame Curie,
I do not remember it. Terror is air-borne.
And though I have been slow to believe,

so are wisdom and beauty, the breath
of canticle and rain forest, and in such
measure as dwarfs the one or two
dark, burrowing parts per million of all
that is our phenomenal inheritance. How

I wish now a teacher had told us that this
is the reason, when we hyperventilate,
we get so dizzy — so much goodness
flooding our little brains it very nearly
bowls us over, tips us toward our knees.

MAJOR JACKSON

from *Urban Renewal*

XIX

That moment in church when I stared at the reverend's black
kente-paneled robe & sash, his right hand clasping the back
of my neck, the other seizing my forehead, standing
in his *Watch this* pose, a leg behind him ready to spring,
his whole body leaning into the salvation of my wizened soul,
I thought of the Saturday morning wrestlers of my youth who'd hold
their opponents till they collapsed on a canvas in a slumberous
heap, and how it looked more like a favor, a deed, though barbarous,
a graceful tour out of this world, that chthonic departure
back to first waters, and wondered what pains I endured
in Mr. Feltyburger's physic's class, worshipping light, density, mass,
preferring to stare long at snowdomes or the carcasses
of flies pooling above in the great fluorescent cover, and how beds
are graves, my mother and father kissing each other's head,
their cupped faces unhurriedly laying the other down,
and how all locked embraces light in my mind from below
in blue-neon like you'd find on the undercarriage of sports cars,
and then what came was the baker stacking her loaves,

one by one, into little coffers, and Desdemona's
last surrender to Othello's piercing glance, and Isaac shown
a militia of clouds over Moriah, and the dying we submerge
in a baptism of pillows, and how we always loiter at this verge,
there, between rising up and falling back, as in now, this tank
of sound I swim in, gripped between the push and yank
of his clutch, caught in that rush of tambourines next to solemn
trays of grape juice and bits of crackers held by deacons when
the reverend, serious as a pew, whispered, "Fall back, my son. Fall."

LILY PRESS

All Natural Drunkard

Possessive
to the last drop
of corn-whiskey stillness
Brewed in the backwoods
of wide-open spaces
Star-dappled moonshine
from the still
of nature's warehouse
Fermented in a black-hole sun
of all alone
Seasoned with the heady scream of vulture
Mixed with coyote's mournful howl
A leaking
barrel of solitude
that drop by drop
becomes an ocean
of sober tranquility

156

Nunca Tu Alma

I turn my eyes from the girls' thin bodies
in Sarajevo and from corpses that float down river
like matchsticks, but here in the clinic
I sit with Maya — a twelve-year-old, raped
by her sister's friend — who asks me, *Am I still a virgin?*
I examine her crimson vagina. Three
delicate tears lace her perineum, as if Maya
has had a rough delivery.
I culture for GC, chlamydia, draw blood
for pregnancy, HIV.
Am I still a virgin? she asks, her voice disembodied
above her knees, bent and open,
her hips narrow as a boy's beneath the sheet.
I struggle with mechanical *vs.* emotional, consider
the penis as metaphor. When we're finished,
Maya and I lean close, face to face.
Virginity is a matter of love, I say, when you give yourself
out of joy. Rape takes only your body, never your soul.
Maya nods, repeats this in Spanish
to her mother and sister, three dark women
singing like birds. Maya imitates me, her fist
strikes her palm: *Nunca, nunca tu alma.*
Her tests are negative.
Maya's more like thirty than twelve,
the nurse whispers, and I agree.
I crumple the sheet and dump the bloody swabs.
Shove the metal stirrups into the table, out of sight.

2006

It was a rainy evening in the garden,
perfect since I'm a turtle and my home is a pond.
— Li-Young Lee

Poems selected by Wally Swist
Fresh Voices poem selected by Mimi Madden

Featuring

Jane Hirshfield

Jim Daniels

John Surowiecki (runner-up, Sunken Garden Poetry Prize)

Renée Ashley (winner, Sunken Garden Poetry Prize)

Li-Young Lee

Olivia Ho-Shing (Fresh Voices, The Masters School)

Norah Pollard

Also read: Fresh Voices from Connecticut High Schools
Charlotte Crowe, Canton High School
(also, Greater Hartford Academy of the Arts)
Morgan Enowitch, Cromwell High School
(also, Greater Hartford Academy of the Arts)
Sarah Gardiner, Manchester High School
(also, Greater Hartford Academy of the Arts)
Lauren Schwartzman, Canton High School
(also, Greater Hartford Academy of the Arts)

The Bell Zygmunt

For fertility, a new bride is lifted to touch it with her left hand,
or possibly kiss it.
The sound close in, my friend told me later, is almost silent.

At ten kilometers even those who have never heard it know what it is.

If you stand near during thunder, she said,
you will hear a reply.

Six weeks and six days from the phone's small ringing,
replying was over.

She who cooked lamb and loved wine and wild-mushroom pastas.
She who when I saw her last was silent as the great Zygmunt mostly is.
A ventilator's clapper between her dry lips.

Because I could, I spoke. She laid her palm on my cheek to answer.
And soon again, to say it was time to leave.

I put my lips near the place a tube went into
the back of one hand.

The kiss — as if it knew what I did not yet — both full and formal.

As one would kiss the ring of a cardinal, or the rim
of that cold iron bell, whose speech can mean "Great joy,"
or — equally — "The city is burning. Come."

You bring out the boring white guy in me

you bring out the boring white guy in me
the Ward Cleaver in me. The Pat Boone
in me. The K-Mart in me. The Slurpee
in me. The boiled hotdog in me. The mac
and cheese in me. The Tang in me.
You bring out the Hamburger Helper
in me. You bring out the Twinkie
in me. The Cheez Whiz in me.
You bring out the bowling trophy
in me. The student council in me.
The parliamentary procedure in me.
The missionary position in me.
You bring out the canned vegetables
in me. The Jell-o in me. The training
wheels in me. You bring out
the lawn edger in me. The fast-food
drive-thru window in me. The Valu
Meal in me. You bring out the white
briefs in me. You bring out
the cheap beer and weak coffee
in me. You bring out the 15%
tip chart in me. The sad overweight
weekend golfer in me. You bring out
the ex-smoker in me. The jumper
cables in the trunk with flares
and the red flag to tie to the window
in me. You bring out the Tony Orlando
in me. The canned situation comedy
laughter in me. The elevator music
in me. You bring out the medley
of TV commercial jingles in me.
The Up with People in me.
I've come to a complete stop

at the stop sign. I've got my
emergency flashers on. My doors
are locked, baby,
I'm waiting for you.

JOHN SUROWIECKI

Bolivia Street

It's the last of the nation streets. After it
are the tree streets and then the president streets.
When it gets paved, shoes and lungs
get brushed with tar and the low-hanging
leaves of maple and oak get cooked.

Barney says there's nothing there anymore:
no candy store, no theater, no bakery,
no tailor shop displaying a boy's hound's-

tooth jacket with leather shank buttons.
The metal shop is a graveyard of parts.
The war plaque has no room for new names.

And since the bees have disappeared
the azaleas suffer and the thyme is winter-quiet.
Each house wears the face of someone old
and failing and shadows of airplanes dart
from roof to roof like angels of death.

What She Wanted

> A sudden blow: the great wings beating still . . .
> —Yeats, "Leda and the Swan"

Not what you think. She imagined
love, yes, and the wings thrashing

with the force of it, white feathers,
white water, flashing all around,

and the breath at her neck, like a blade's
keen side, one edge of his shameless

desire. And hers, she will tell you,
like a deft honing in cool water. She wanted him

like that. And she wanted him to risk
any small thing—his life, for instance,

if that were possible—to possess her.
She wanted him to traverse oceans, cross

silver bodies of perilous water; she wanted
him reflected there, and vulnerable—blind

to all but fierce need and the brave wind
teasing her hair; she wanted him unaware of wave

and precipitous rock. And she liked the word
tread, the idea of the watery fuck—

the cool shade at the steep, muddy banks
and the current in between. She wanted him

to own all that: the depths of need
and the body's fallible knowledge.

How far one might go for love,
and the waters one crosses to get there.

LI-YOUNG LEE

Immigrant Blues

People have been trying to kill me since I was born,
a man tells his son, trying to explain
the wisdom of learning a second tongue.

It's an old story from the previous century
about my father and me.

The same old story from yesterday morning
about me and my son.

It's called "Survival Strategies
and the Melancholy of Racial Assimilation."

It's called "Psychological Paradigms of Displaced Persons,"

called "The Child Who'd Rather Play than Study."

Practice until you feel
the language inside you, says the man.

But what does he know about inside and outside,
my father who was spared nothing
in spite of the languages he used?

And me, confused about the flesh and the soul,
who asked once into a telephone,
Am I inside you?

You're always inside me, a woman answered,
at peace with the body's finitude,
at peace with the soul's disregard
of space and time.

Am I inside you? I asked once
lying between her legs, confused
about the body and the heart.

If you don't believe you're inside me, you're not,
she answered, at peace with the body's greed,
at peace with the heart's bewilderment.

It's an ancient story from yesterday evening

called "Patterns of Love in Peoples of Diaspora,"

called "Loss of the Homeplace
and the Defilement of the Beloved,"

called "I Want to Sing but I Don't Know Any Songs."

.

OLIVIA HO-SHING

As a Poet

I am a starling runt with broken wing,
A fish swimming in Jell-o,
A garbage can.
An echo that scarcely returns,
One chopstick.
I've smoked a cigar that lingers with bitterness.
I am linoleum flooring, mouth in foot.
A blind dog fathoming the universe in howls.
I have sucked from earth and I am still not ripe.

Last Light

If, some summer evening,
you were to come upon
my father's bones
under the ferns
by the dark and languid
Ten Mile River,
you would find them small,
for a man,
and note that the skull
was beautifully shaped.

You would note, too,
the unusually long and
narrow bones of his hands
bound together by the black rosary,
the fine shreds of green silk tie
still caught around the white
spools of his neck, and
the hair, translucent when
they buried him, now
perfectly clear, luminous as
spider's silk.

Many of his bones would show
old cracks and fractures —
his nose, ribs, one arm, a hand,
the hips, that terrible leg, the clavicle —
a chronicle of bad breaks
in a life of riding horses.

And then, if you were to kneel
and hold back the laurel and blackthorn
shading what had been his face,

you would find,
pooled in its socket like
a tiny lake among snow hills,
his glass eye,
steadfastly shining,
eternally innocent of the wild, harsh,
and gorgeous world it had gazed upon,
forever blue.

2008

As close to a perfect, serene, ecstatic experience as I can imagine.
—Coleman Barks

Poems selected by Brad Davis
Connecticut Poetry Circuit poem selected by Amy Russo
Fresh Voices poem selected by Mimi Madden

Featuring

Robert Pinsky

Tyler Theofilos (Connecticut Poetry Circuit, Yale University)

Coleman Barks

Billy Collins

Patricia Fargnoli

Ilya Kaminsky

Paul Muldoon

Sasha Debevec-McKenney (Fresh Voices, Windsor High School;

also, Greater Hartford Academy of the Arts)

Also read: Fresh Voices from Connecticut High Schools
Britta Bell, Litchfield High School
(also, Greater Hartford Academy of the Arts)
Jameson Fitzpatrick, Simsbury High School
(also, Greater Hartford Academy of the Arts)
Hannah Loeb, Kingswood Oxford School
Nicole Marella, Ellington High School

Connecticut Poetry Circuit
Tess Bird, University of Connecticut
Lisa Butler, Manchester Community College
Chiara Di Lello, Wesleyan University
Taylor Katz, Connecticut College

Poem of Disconnected Parts

At Robben Island the political prisoners studied.
They coined the motto *Each one Teach one.*

In Argentina the torturers demanded the prisoners
Address them always as "*Profesor.*"

Many of my friends are moved by guilt, but I
Am a creature of shame, I am ashamed to say.

Culture the lock, culture the key. Imagination
That calls boiled sheep heads "Smileys."

The first year at Guantánamo, Abdul Rahim Dost
Incised his Pashto poems into styrofoam cups.

"*The Sangomo says in our Zulu culture we do not
Worship our ancestors: we consult them.*"

Becky is abandoned in 1902 and Rose dies giving
Birth in 1924 and Sylvia falls in 1951.

Still falling still dying still abandoned in 2005
Still nothing finished among the descendants.

I support the War, says the comic, it's just the Troops
I'm against: can't stand those Young People.

Proud of the fallen, proud of her son the bomber.
Ashamed of the government. Skeptical.

After the Klansman was found Not Guilty one juror
Said she just couldn't vote to convict a pastor.

Who do you write for? I write for dead people:
For Emily Dickinson, for my grandfather.

"The Ancestors say the problem with your Knees
Began in your Feet. It could move up your Back."

But later the Americans gave Dost not only paper
And pen but books. Hemingway, Dickens.

Old Aegyptius said Whoever has called this Assembly,
For whatever reason — it is a good in itself.

O thirsty shades who regard the offering, O stained earth.
There are many fake Sangomos. This one is real.

Coloured prisoners got different meals and could wear
Long pants and underwear, Blacks got only shorts.

No he says he cannot regret the three years in prison:
Otherwise he would not have written those poems.

I have a small-town mind. Like the Greeks and Trojans.
Shame. Pride. Importance of looking bad or good.

Did he see anything like the prisoner on a leash? Yes,
In Afghanistan. In Guantánamo he was isolated.

Our enemies "disassemble" says the President.
Not that anyone at all couldn't mis-speak.

The *profesores* created nicknames for torture devices:
The Airplane. The Frog. Burping the Baby.

Not that those who behead the helpless in the name
Of God or tradition don't also write poetry.

Guilts, metaphors, traditions. Hunger strikes.
Culture the penalty. Culture the escape.

What could your children boast about you? What
Will your father say, down among the shades?

The Sangomo told Marvin, *"You are crushed by some
Weight. Only your own Ancestors can help you."*

TYLER THEOFILOS

Night Drive

Everything was like listening to the radio
until I heard the radio for the first time.
I was watching the snow through the window,
and the sound of it was enormous.
Colonies of flakes fell in
and dove up at every moment.
Venus was somehow perched
in the white arms of each birch
until it looked silly.
I couldn't realize anything then,
but the night was no less a thing than I was a thing,
than Venus was a thing and not just a word,
than the living snow dove up as just a thing.
My life was always a life of surfaces.
You, too, were a surface of waiting snow
before I came along and watched you.
Sometimes we are told this,
and sometimes we are shown this.
Usually, though, it is something between the two.
Usually, the red parenthesis of leaves appears
on one lawn, then three, then all of them.

What Was Said to the Rose

What was said to the rose that made it open
was said to me here in my chest.

What was told the Cypress that made it strong
and straight, what was

whispered the jasmine so it is what it is, whatever made
sugarcane sweet, whatever

was said to the inhabitants of the town of Chigil in
Turkestan that makes them

so handsome, whatever lets the pomegranate flower blush
like a human face, that is

being said to me now. I blush. Whatever put eloquence in
language, that's happening here.

The great warehouse doors open; I fill with gratitude,
chewing a piece of sugarcane,

in love with the one to whom every that belongs!

by Jalaluddin Rumi, translated by Coleman Barks

The Lanyard

The other day I was ricocheting slowly
off the blue walls of this room,
moving as if underwater from typewriter to piano,
from bookshelf to an envelope lying on the floor,
when I found myself in the L section of the dictionary
where my eyes fell upon the word lanyard.

No cookie nibbled by a French novelist
could send one into the past more suddenly —
a past where I sat at a workbench at a camp
by a deep Adirondack lake
learning how to braid long thin plastic strips
into a lanyard, a gift for my mother.

I had never seen anyone use a lanyard
or wear one, if that's what you did with them,
but that did not keep me from crossing
strand over strand again and again
until I had made a boxy
red and white lanyard for my mother.

She gave me life and milk from her breasts,
and I gave her a lanyard.
She nursed me in many a sick room,
lifted spoons of medicine to my lips,
laid cold face-cloths on my forehead,
and then led me out into the airy light

and taught me to walk and swim,
and I, in turn, presented her with a lanyard.
Here are thousands of meals, she said,
and here is clothing and a good education.
And here is your lanyard, I replied,
which I made with a little help from a counselor.

Here is a breathing body and a beating heart,
strong legs, bones and teeth,
and two clear eyes to read the world, she whispered,
and here, I said, is the lanyard I made at camp.
And here, I wish to say to her now,
is a smaller gift—not the worn truth

that you can never repay your mother,
but the rueful admission that when she took
the two-tone lanyard from my hand,
I was as sure as a boy could be
that this useless, worthless thing I wove
out of boredom would be enough to make us even.

PATRICIA FARGNOLI

Duties of the Spirit

> *one of the duties of the spirit is joy, and another is serenity.*
> —Thorton Wilder in a letter to Paul Stephenson, 1930

If the first is joy—
the rhumba at sunrise,
a three-note whistle in the sugar maple—

and the second is serenity—
a chair by a quiet window,
the wind fading down the hill at sleep—

then the third must be grief—
rock-tight, then loosening like scarves the wind takes
across the ocean while on the shore
the shells' empty houses lie scattered.

And if the first is in the brief seconds
which are all we can keep of happiness—

and if the second waits alone in the hour
where the pond smoothes out, its surface
unbroken and the moon in it —

then the third which is grief comes again and again
longer and more than we wanted
or ever wished for

to wash us clean with its saltwater,
to empty our throats, and fill them
again with bloodroot song.

And if the first
duty of the spirit is leaping joy,
and the second
the slow stroll of serenity,

then grief, the third, comes bending on his walking stick,
holding a trowel to dig where the loves have gone,

and he weighs down your shoulders, ties a rawhide necklace
hung with a stone around your neck, and hangs on and on.

But the first is slippery joy.

ILYA KAMINSKY

Maestro

What is memory? what makes a body glow:
an apple orchard in Moldova and the school is bombed —

when the schools are bombed, sadness is forbidden
—I write this now and I feel my body's weight:

the screaming girls, 347 voices
in the story of a doctor saving them, his hands

trapped under a wall, his granddaughter dying nearby —
she whispers *I don't want to die, I have eaten such apples.*

He watches her mouth as a blind man reading lips
and yells *Shut up! I am near the window, I*

am asking for help! speaking,
he cannot stop speaking, in the dark:

of Brahms, Chopin he speaks to them to calm them.
A doctor, yes, whatever window

framed his life, outside: tomatoes grew, clouds passed and we
once lived. A doctor with a tattoo of a parrot on his trapped arm,

seeing his granddaughter's cheekbones
no longer her cheekbones, with surgical precision

stitches suffering and grace:
two days pass, he shouts

in his window (there is no window) when rescue
approaches, he speaks of Chopin, Chopin.

They cut off his hands, nurses say he is "doing OK"
— in my dream: he stands, feeding bread to pigeons, surrounded

by pigeons, birds on his head, his shoulder,
he shouts *You don't understand a thing!*

he is breathing himself to sleep, the city sleeps,
there is no such city.

The Mountain Is Holding Out

The mountain is holding out
for news from the sea
and the raid on the redoubt.
The plain won't level with me

for news from the sea
is harder and harder to find.
The plain won't level with me
now it's non-aligned

and harder and harder to find.
The forest won't fill me in
now it, too, is non-aligned
and its patience wearing thin.

The forest won't fill me in
nor the lake confess
to its patience wearing thin.
I'd no more try to second guess

why the lake would confess
to its regard for its own sheen,
no more try to second guess
why the river won't come clean

on its regard for its own sheen
than why you and I've faced off across a ditch.
For the river not coming clean
is only one of the issues on which

you and I've faced off across a ditch
and the raid on the redoubt
only one of the issues on which
the mountain is holding out.

what i left on capen street

my mother,
half of my brother,
the clothes i don't fit into anymore,
my truancy,
a front yard whose
snow i don't have to shovel anymore
because i live in an apartment
with my dad —
he leaves
and i clean out the dishwasher,
he comes home
and i go upstairs,
and it feels sort of like i'm living by myself,
which at least feels better than
feeling like living with only half of myself.

i left more than
everything that got pushed under my bed,
more than walking to school whenever i felt like it.
i left because i needed to
to put my feet down
on the same carpet every morning,
to the left of the same
diet coke stain and
not to leave
every four days,
come back from capen
to find my alarm clock unplugged,
again.

the part of my brain that remembered
what heap of clothes my cell phone charger was under
is free to remember so much more useful things, like
woodrow wilson quotes and
rod carew's lifetime batting average, and
when that math project is due.
all my socks are in one place,
everything finally makes a pair.

when i was on capen street last week,
stuffing everything that couldn't be left
into black garbage bags,
i found that orange shirt i love
and it fits into a space the perfect size for it
in my bureau at my dad's house,
its way of telling me how much it enjoys
finally being part of a real wardrobe
for the first time in its lonely, orange life.

and even though it's awkward
and rushed
and i try to forget
and i fumble,
most of what i left on capen street
is my mother —
who built fires in the fireplace
and let me sleep until two in the afternoon on Saturdays
and i keep wondering if this
feels to her like
giving birth to me for the second time.

2009

*Sitting with their evening picnics, opening themselves
to the mysteries of poetry in such a generous way,
the audience is one of the best in America.*
—Brenda Hillman

Poems selected by Jim Finnegan
Cave Canem poem selected by Brad Davis
Connecticut Poetry Circuit poem selected by Amy Russo
Fresh Voices poem selected by Mimi Madden

Featuring

Robert Hass

Brenda Hillman

Susanna Myserth (Connecticut Poetry Circuit, Wesleyan University)

Baron Wormser

Martina Crouch (Fresh Voices, Danbury High School)

Kim Roberts (winner, Sunken Garden Poetry Prize)

Lita Hooper (Cave Canem)

Marilyn Nelson

Don Thompson (runner-up, Sunken Garden Poetry Prize)

C. K. Williams

Also read: Fresh Voices from Connecticut High Schools
Charlotte Beach, Wilbur Cross High School
Emily Delano, Hall High School
Alexander Guarco, E. O. Smith High School
Melanie Lieberman, Rockville High School

Connecticut Poetry Circuit
Matthew Gilbert, University of Hartford
Jordan Jacks, Yale University
Sarah Nichols, Tunxis Community College
Katie Rowe, Albertus Magnus College

Cave Canem Poets
Opal Palmer Adisa
Carleasa Coates
John Murillo

from *August Notebook: A Death*

4.

Today his body is consigned to the flames
and I begin to understand why people
would want to carry a body to the river's edge
and build a platform of wood and burn it
in the wind and scatter the ashes in the river.
As if to say, take him, fire, take him, air,
and, river, take him. Downstream. Downstream.
Watch the ashes disappear in the fast water
or, in a small flaring of anger, turn away, walk back
toward the markets and the hum of life, not quite
saying to yourself *There, the hell with it, it's done.*
I said to him once, when he'd gotten into some scrape
or other, "You know, you have the impulse control
of a ferret." And he said, "Yeah? I don't know
what a ferret is, but I get greedy. I don't mean to,
but I get greedy." An old grubber's beard, going grey,
a wheelchair, sweats, a street person's baseball cap.
"I've been thinking about Billie Holiday, you know
if she were around now, she'd be nothing. You know
what I mean? Hip-hop? Never. She had to be born
at a time when they were writing the kind of songs
and people were listening to the kind of songs
she was great at singing." And I would say,
"You just got evicted from your apartment,
you can't walk, and you have no money, so
I don't want to talk to you about Billie Holiday
right now, OK." And he would say, "You know,
I'm like Mom. I mean, she really had a genius
for denial, don't you think? And the thing is,
you know, she was a pretty happy person."
And I would say, "She was not a happy person.

She was panicky and crippled by guilt at her drinking,
hollowed out by it, honeycombed with it,
and she was evasive to herself about herself,
and so she couldn't actually connect with anybody,
and her only defense was to be chronically cheerful."
And he would say, "Worse things than cheerful."
Well, I am through with those arguments,
except in my head, though I seem not to be through with the habit—
I thought this poem would end *downstream downstream*—
of worrying about where you are and how you're doing.

BRENDA HILLMAN

The Late Cold War

A man says he doesn't understand my poetry

Frankly i'm not surprised

I learned to write in a hot desert during the cold war
We did air raid drills in a schoolyard full of thick-skinned
    ornamental oranges

We saw dioramas of a fall-out shelter where a mother wearing a light
    print housedress served t.v. dinners on aluminum trays to children
    wearing saddle shoes

The man says poetry should be simple enough
    for school girls to understand

But sir, school girls understand everything

Nancy Drew was in love with the obstacle not the clue

My near-sighted eyes had adjusted to reading & by 1962
letters had developed fuzzy antennas like tarantulas or modernism

The psyche rises like mist from things, writes Heraclitus

Sir, when i think of poetry keeping you alive i know
   you were entered by incomprehensible light
   in the hour of lemon & water

& the great wound of the world has slipped a code
   into your shoe

A poem doesn't fail when you set your one good wing on the ground

It is the wing
It doesn't abandon you

SUSANNA MYSERTH

First Try

It began so well: first I built time,
shook out the universe like a crisp cotton sheet and let it settle,
named the days so I could peel light from dark on a Tuesday.
I liked the sound of that—like biting into something
taut and nearly saline. I made citrus fruit on Tuesday evening,
a side project so fun I spent all of Wednesday on plants,
realized I had nowhere to put them
and made the world.

There is nothing linear about creation.
No momentum of reason can outweigh whim stoked with power—
I was drunk with it. This shaping.
I had no body to burst with pride
so each thing I made was a new nerve ending.
The stars I claimed as teeth,
one mountain as a freckle on my nonexistent elbow.
Unconstrained by reality or proportion, how big would you be?

By Saturday I lacked only a tongue.
Nothing held the right weight or texture.
I had never seen a tongue,
only possessed the vaguest sense that it went
somewhere between the stars and my appetite.

Knowing that, I breathed you out, almost choked in the process,
your flesh formed to lend shape to my humming.
You are all noise and no echo,
long muscle, short memory
and what I meant to say was take it easy.
Build up your baby bones slow like calcium collecting
at the bottom of the ocean.
Your cheeks were as small as fish scales.
I was startled by the thinness of your arms.

You were not what I expected but
I am not what I expected either.
I never saw my own face until I made eyes and a mirror,
until I invented seeing.

So don't believe what they tell you — on Sunday I found no rest.
Instead I trembled, an insect suspended
in a web of my own spinning,
watching every atom heave and sigh,
attempting to get the measure of my breath.

BARON WORMSER

My Last Borders, or
Poem Ending with a Homage to W. B. Yeats

Once I read in a Borders Bookstore
In a sea of shopping malls in New Jersey.
A man sat in the first row and pawed over
The poems he was going to read later during the open mic.

He never looked up at me but snorted occasionally
With vatic delight at his own precipitous genius.
The espresso machine in the rear of the café
Made troubled basso sounds like a dying cow.

I read in the café because the "events area"
Was hosting a talk on "Planning a Trust Fund."
My books for sale were under a table on which a slide
Projector sat and showed screens like "Your House—
Your Greatest Asset" and "Tomorrow Does Come."

A woman in the third row (there were only three rows)
Talked intermittently on a cell phone to someone named Yvette:
"Are you really staying in a hotel, Yvette?"
"You can get that much cheaper in Paramus."
"I can't believe you're still seeing that loser."
When people told her to be quiet, she said
That she liked to talk and listen to poetry
At the same time. She said it was "multi-sensory."
After the reading she came up to me and told me
She thought I was going to be a hick from Maine
But I turned out to be a Jewish intellectual.
She informed me that she was Jewish too that novelists were smarter
Than poets and that she had been to Europe eight times.
After the events director crawled under the Trust
Planning Table and brought my latest title back to the café,
She bought one of the two books that were sold that evening.

How sad am I to do these readings?
Just normal-aching-poet-sad?
Delmore-Schwartz-cornered-by-the-abyss sad?
Or cowardly? Afraid to be Sylvia-Plath-angry-sad
And barge through death's sullen door,
Sick of human idiocy, including my own?

Later in the evening when I have repaired
To the poetry section to gather my slender wits,
I consult the oracle Yeats.

He never drove on Interstates among convoys of 18-wheelers,
Never searched asphalt acres for a parking space
Around Christmas, never took a self-assertion seminar
Or credit management workshop in a fluorescent warehouse.
The chains of commerce never danced for him.

He stood for the soul's exactions, the flawed
Avid beauty of conscience. I read his poems
And feel better, which is to say, sadder.

MARTINA CROUCH

Summersick

I miss the way it comes:
as a smell, on curved feet,
a sliver of apple.
The way it unfurls from students' lips:
summer.
I thrive on summer. I live.
I miss the way the days
stumble over each other in waves,
fast and warm like a pulse,
and I miss the hungry marketplace
that gorges itself on fruit;
the way the leaves swallow people whole-heartedly
into silence.
I miss the little white wildflowers
I crush beneath my feet, the
dandelions scorching tiny suns
into glassy-eyed
sky.
I remember most the way it leaves:
cooling sweat from sultry skin
in a barely whispered apology;
tingeing

leaves
orange,
sucking soil dry,
leaving in the middle of the stagnant, dreamless night,
so that the garden dies before it ever begins,
and cherry blossoms sprawl like
dead ballerinas in the dirt,
and the cicadas
forget how to sing.

KIM ROBERTS

My Imaginary Husband

My husband always talks
         about the wind
      that shakes up the trees;

he's got sixteen
         different ways to describe
      how the leaves chatter.

I can think of
         a half dozen sounds
      I'd rather hear.

But my husband is always
         most joyful
      when everything looms.

He dances in splayed sneakers
         across asphalt's brittle trust
      while the trees declaim,

wagging their fingers,
        and the alley's loose chain link
   rattles like a guard dog.

When everything looms —
        a storm, a fight —
   my husband is bouyant;

he loves most the frayed
        and dangerous edges
   that threaten to call us out of our names.

LITA HOOPER

Ellipse

a poem for Martin Luther King, Jr.

I

The sun crouched behind skyscrapers
as my father's curveballs met
the thin leather of my old mitt.
Between each pitch, his commentary rose
above street noise and the blaring radio
from the house next door.
        Your fastball looks good, Martin.
        But it's the curveball that'll
        win you the game.
He kept 'em coming, each ball aimed
at my heart. Before long
his arms, legs, and face disappeared
one at a time
as darkness settled between us.
I turned around to answer the call —
my mother's silhouette in the window.

II

The doors flew open to
Ebeneezer Baptist Church
devouring each eager-eyed congregant.
I could hear the longing chords of an organ
as we two-stepped forward. My mother's hand
released my sweaty grip. I remained
pressed between overcoats and handbags.
When I returned, there was only the familiar
pale blue sky peering through
slightly bowed fedoras.

III

I can't remember the color of her dress
or if it was sunny that day we walked across
her campus. I can't tell you if my arm
brushed hers
or even if she made it to class on time.
I can only recall looking up at her
as she reached the last stair
her beautiful hand reaching for the door
a quick turn, then her smile
like dawn breaking
as the world graciously paused.
Years later I would return
to Coretta's smile—
a compass for my travel-weary heart.

IV

The black and white footage
casts us in courage
elbows locked in our audacity.
Photos of that day read brave
but film cannot capture
a rapid pulse hidden beneath coats
and stoic stares. I suppose we forgot
for a moment

how cold it was as we turned
toward the impartial bridge.
It did not judge us
or cheer us toward its iron heights.

v

I don't know what can be said
of this life we all share
the timely defeats and insignificant
victories that add up
to a day, a month, a lifetime.
I only know that life is an ellipse
each of us equal at each turn.

MARILYN NELSON

Aubade (Dawn Song)

(1768)

Started out early, following last night's track.
A moon sliver lingered over the moon blue snow.
I left my lady laying on her back
trumpeting the most beautiful music I know.
Can't take her home with me, where she belongs,
to warm my room with her smile, my pillow with her cheek.
She and our children: owned. (God must bear wrongs
like a strong black man pretending to be meek.)
Like me, my Meg was kidnapped as a child
and raised in a white home, the only slave.
We are resurrecting the portions of us killed,
inventing together a language to express love.
Sometimes we whisper words lost long ago.
I'd rather be with her now than out here
        in this god-forsaken snow.

Where We Live

Nocturnal creatures must teach their young
to be heard and not seen.
Coyotes yip to the east of us
and to the west, frogs beat their drums.

Somewhere to the south, a bird calls—
two thin, falling syllables
in a language we'll never know,
except for rough translations into loneliness.

Where we live, you have to listen hard
through cricket static to hear yourself think.
I like that. For once,
everything human has to shut up and sit still.

You can't even hear the traffic on I5,
only a few miles to the northeast,
where big rigs drift by like ghosts with lanterns
trapped in a long, dark hallway.

The Coffin Store

I was lugging my death from Kampala to Krakow.
Death, what a ridiculous load you can be,
like the world trembling on Atlas's shoulders.

In Kampala I'd wondered why the people, so poor,
didn't just kill me. Why don't they kill me?
In Krakow I must have fancied I'd find poets to talk to.

I still believed then I'd domesticated my death,
that he'd no longer gnaw off my fingers and ears.
We even had parties together: "Happy," said death,

and gave me my present, a coffin, my coffin,
made in Kampala, with a sliding door in its lid,
to look through, at the sky, at the birds, at Kampala.

That was his way, I soon understood, of reverting
to talon and snarl, for the door refused to come open:
no sky, no bird, no poets, no Krakow.

Catherine came to me then, came to me then,
"Open your eyes, mon amour," but death
had undone me, my knuckles were raw as an ape's,

my mind slid like a sad-ankled skate, and no matter
what Catherine was saying, was sighing, was singing,
"Mon amour, mon amour," the door stayed shut, oh, shut.

I heard trees being felled, skinned, smoothed,
hammered together as coffins. I heard death
snorting and stamping, impatient to be hauled off, away.

But here again was Catherine, sighing, and singing,
and the tiny carved wooden door slid ajar, just enough:
the sky, one single bird, Catherine: just enough.

2010

*Whether listening to young poets in high school or college, or a
Poet Laureate of the United States, there is magic here—as sheep bawl
out in the field, and the moon slowly rises above the treetops.*
—Ginny Lowe Connors

Poems selected by Norah Pollard
Connecticut Poetry Circuit poem selected by Amy Russo
Fresh Voices poem selected by Mimi Madden

Featuring

Galway Kinnell

Bessy Reyna

Gabrielle Calvocoressi

Kate Lebo (runner-up, Sunken Garden Poetry Prize)

Ginny Connors (winner, Sunken Garden Poetry Prize)

Jean Valentine

Kristin Rocha (Connecticut Poetry Circuit, Trinity College)

Terrance Hayes

Victoria Chen (Fresh Voices, E. O. Smith High School)

Taylor Mali

Also read: Fresh Voices from Connecticut High Schools
Megan Brookman, Farmington High School
(also, Greater Hartford Academy of the Arts)
Andrew Bryce, E. O. Smith High School
Elizabeth Nutt, Rockville High School
Kerrylee Pelkey, Bacon Academy
Machael Stankiewicz, Rockville High School

Connecticut Poetry Circuit
John Dudek, University of Hartford
Katherine Orazem, Yale University
Caitlin Scott, Connecticut College

It All Comes Back

We placed the cake, with its four candles
poking out of thick soft frosting, on the seat
of his chair at the head of the table
for just a moment, while we unfolded and spread
Spanish cloth over Vermont maple.

Suddenly he stepped from the group
of schoolmates and parents and family friends
and ran to the table, and just as someone cried
No, no! Don't sit! he sat on his chair and his cake,
and the room broke into groans and guffaws.

Actually it was pretty funny, we all
started yelping our heads off, and actually
it wasn't in the least funny. He ran to me,
and I picked him up but I was still laughing,
and in indignant fury he jabbed his thumbs

into the corners of my mouth, grasped
my cheeks, and yanked—he was so muscled
and so outraged I felt as if he might rip
my whole face off, and then I realized
that was exactly what he was trying to do.

It came to me: I was one of his keepers,
his birth and the birth of his sister
had put me on earth a second time,
with the duty this time to protect them
and to help them to love themselves,

and yet here I was, locked in solidarity
with these adults against my own child,
hee-hawing away, without once wondering
if we weren't, underneath, all of us, striking back,
too late, at our parents for humiliating us.

I gulped down my laughter and held him and
apologized and commiserated and explained and then
things were right again, but to this day it remains
loose, this face, seat of superior smiles,
on the bones, from that hard yanking.

Shall I publish this anecdote from the past
and risk embarrassing him? I like it
that he fought back, but what's the good,
now he's thirty-six, in telling the tale
of his mortification when he was four?

Let him decide—I'll give him three choices.
He can scratch his slapdash checkmark,
whose rakish hook reminds me
of his old high-school hockey stick,
in whichever box applies:

❐ *Tear it up.*   ❐ *Don't publish it but give me a copy.*
❐ *O.K. publish it on the off chance that*
somewhere someone survives
of those said to die miserably every day
for lack of the small clarifications sometimes found in poems.

BESSY REYNA

The Ukiyo-e *Lady in the Snow*

from a painting by Kikugawa Eizan (1787–1867)

In the middle of the storm
the red umbrella keeps the snow away from her face.

She is Eizan's *ukiyo-e* lady
sentenced to stand in the harbor forever.

Hair pulled back, waist tied by an obi,
she turns her back to the sea.

This winter morning how I want to look like her,
the elegant stance, the perfect neck.

Hear the wind fondle the black and gold kimono
as I stand barefoot in the snow.

GABRIELLE CALVOCORESSI

Every Person in This Town Loves Football

Even the nuns come out
to watch the boys in their
gold and blue. Sister Marita,
Sister Anne and some weeks

Sister Perpetua who still
uses the ruler on our outstretched
hands. Even the mills
get quiet and how

the new freeway subsides
for awhile so we almost
remember the fields
full of tobacco and feed

corn, the older kids
sent out to harvest alongside
those men who'd come up
from the South. *It's hard*

on the hands my babysitter
told me and showed the small
cuts like netting placed over
the palm. She'd calm me

down when I woke or I'd come
downstairs to find her splayed
out on the couch, head thrown
back and Keith, our quarterback,

working above her. Everybody
loves that sound: all the breath
sucked out of the town and just
as quickly it roars back in,

his arm tensed and stuttering
till he just lets go. From the arm,
from the start of the arc and now
over the heads of Beckett and Pulaski,

over the girls in their short short skirts
to the place where the blast furnace
meets the darkness. Who's your daddy?
If he lived in this town he played

the game too and every girl
held his name in her mouth.
He wore dress shirts on game day
with a tie and his jersey

on top. He walked down the halls
smelling of Old Spice and chew.
Who could break a boy like that?
Who could grind his smallest bones

or show him the bars where men spill
out of their worn letter jackets.
Come Friday we'll turn the lights on.
You'll see us from everywhere.

Happy Birthday

Another November
off my list. What's left?
Damp laundry, your
hesitating kiss.
My egg breath
and shoehorn thighs.
I've leaned your name
in my mouth
like a rake,
and tallied all
the dependable
things:

tap water, junk mail,
the rough shade you cast
when I turn my head just so
to the left, the rag
stuffed beneath my dish rack,
half-black and blurred as a rubbed eye,
the stains bearding the bathroom
window and the sky.

I'm still renting my pay from the city.
Still reading the Times
like a barcode. No smarter
than I started,
but no more guilty than a bathrobe.

Duty is still my body
catching the 49 bus,
patience is the paint chip
in the white kitchen wall
where a square of red

blinks like a brake light
and habit,

if we have it,
is your toothbrush drying
in the short plastic cup.
Behind the house a hubbub
of rhubarb
doubles down under the dirt. Your tomatoes
are as green as green grows.

GINNY LOWE CONNORS

Under the Porch

In a drift of sawdust, shadows
and long strands of web,
in the smell of damp,
mineral-laden dirt, that toad

hunched under our porch,
fattened on what black dreams
fell through the cracks.

Daily we walked up the three steps,
over the creaking board and into the house
knowing it was down there,
forgetting it was down there.

Into the soup went the hambone.
Mother stirred while little brother in his corner
cried, his sobs carrying over

the TV's cantata of bad news, canned laughter.
Outside the leaves turned red.
My older brother crouched near me
at the edge of the carport roof, considering

our chances. *You jump first*, he ordered
and so I did. Khaki-colored grass
rose up to greet me and my brother

followed—what choice did he have?
After a hard rain, toad squatted
on the walk, his gnarly skin
like cold sand speckled with gravel.

Evenings, his low croak
traveled up through the floorboards
and into the soles of my feet

as my mother watched the window
turn into a dark mirror,
and my father scraped a match, lit
another Camel. Coughed.

JEAN VALENTINE

Ghost Elephants

In the elephant field
tall green ghost elephants
with your cargo of summer leaves

at night I heard you breathing at the window

Don't you ever think I'm not crying
since you're away from me
Don't ever think I went free

At first the goodbye had a lilt to it—
maybe just a couple of months—
but it was a beheading.

Ghost elephant,
my lost mother,
reach down,
cross me over —

KRISTIN ROCHA

Nationalism

I thought I could never love this city
City of riverbed and cobblestone
Veins moving to and from one another
The caress, the divorce, the caress,
Each finds more agony in the heart
Until finally mountains stand above and seas
Sway below as the city bleeds between.

They call this city Barcelona,
They call it Catalunya, and at night
When everyone sleeps they wash the streets
With river water and collected rain.
The only ones to see are the whores and drunks.

I thought I was not of this city.
The politics of my body parts were not
Assembled, propagandized or marched on here,
Not eclipsed in this language, I wave
No flag but the pendant of my own bones.
Scaffold rising up against the wind
To renovate the problem — the skeletal
Structure sucks my stomach in. And. Up. Braced,
Corseted, I am poised as I move through
These streets like a foreigner, like the heart
That beats because we cannot command it to stop.

I thought I could never love this city
Where roses drip in puddles across
Pavement. Drawing closer they aren't
Petals at all, but blood from the man
Who begs money in the metro and mops
The red pulse with paper.
The tourist upon bending is sickened
By the arena of sidewalk
Lacerations. How lovely it had been,
Just moments before, to think a rose
Had been plucked, disassembled, scattered there.

To run a hand along the tracks that lead out.
Out from the tangle of metro cars,
Out from the taxis, the buses, the beach
With its thieves and imported sand. Fingers
Along the vine to the vineyard, along
The vine to the cava. Standing, looking
Into the sun, it's a flower
With a fertile face and gold plucked to find love.

But the sound of train, the sound of city—
My hand leaves the track and again I am
The ribs (In. And. Up.) The scaffold
Like a cage to renovate and straighten.
I am the streets, the ports, the city.
I am the foreigner, the untrained tongue.
I who ran the street to the sea, to the bones
Of my hips painted thick to say I am
The goddess. I am a goddess, in the
Painting, the picture, the frame with my folds
Of malignant fat. A Rubens muse left
In a city I cannot love
In the body that is the city I cannot
Love. How simple. Remove the performance
Of this fabric to find the threadbare skin
And stand (the shame, the shame) rippled and round
As the curvature of this fountain, this

Bell jar with its tiny dried flowers, pale
And pretty in their fragility. Sick—

It is a fat, soft sickness that traps
The mind inside the body — its tyrant,
Where starving, pleading to get out,
The mind begs bones to show
But the layers, they torment.

There's been a war here, on the backs of hands
In the backs of minds the battle still smarts
And the pull of muscle from bone aches
Like the arm I've just lost to civil dispute,
Always, always within mountain range
Of breasts and belly, ridge of tissue,
Valley of vein, the sea, the sea that spreads
Between parenthetical hips is
The city, Barcelona, Barcelona.

TERRANCE HAYES

Cocktails with Orpheus

After dark, the bar full of women part of me loves — the part that stood
naked outside the window of Miss Geneva, recent divorcée who owned
a gun, O Miss Geneva where are you now — Orpheus says she did

not perish, she was not turned to ash in the brutal light, she found
a good job, she made good money, she had her own insurance and
a house, she was a decent wife. I know descent lives in the word

decent. The bar noise makes a kind of silence. When Orpheus hands
me his sunglasses, I see how fire changes everything. In the mind
I am behind a woman whose skirt is hiked above her hips, as bound

as touch permits, saying don't forget me when I become the liquid
out of which names are born, salt-milk, milk-sweet and animal-made.

I want to be a human above the body, uprooted and right, a fold
of pleas released, but I am a black wound, what's left of the deed.

VICTORIA CHEN

Barbie Gone Conservative

Of all the possible personalities, you, Barbie, will never be a librarian.
Your plastic fingers will never cradle overdue stamps or books on tape.
Your box will never feature make-your-own library cards,
glitter sold separately, barcode not included.

Your shoes will never be that sensible.

Your audience will never let go of that tight bun, tight lipped,
long dress skirt with sneakers stereotype,
and you will never shelve paperbacks or hardcovers,
romances or anthologies.

You will never bring Ken to a hot date at the checkout desk,
never recommend him your latest favorite read,
never look out across glasses propped over your nose
and sigh because, unlike Ken, e.e. cummings took your heart
and Poe sent shivers along your every breath.

Undivided Attention

A grand piano wrapped in quilted pads by movers,
tied up with canvas straps — like classical music's
birthday gift to the insane —
is gently nudged without its legs
out an eighth-floor window on 62nd street.

It dangles in April air from the neck of the movers' crane,
Chopin-shiny black lacquer squares
and dirty white crisscross patterns hanging like the second-to-last
note of a concerto played on the edge of the seat,
the edge of tears, the edge of eight stories up going over, and
I'm trying to teach math in the building across the street.

Who can teach when there are such lessons to be learned?
All the greatest common factors are delivered by
long-necked cranes and flatbed trucks
or come through everything, even air.
Like snow.

See, snow falls for the first time every year, and every year
my students rush to the window
as if snow were more interesting than math,
which, of course, it is.

So please.

Let me teach like a Steinway,
spinning slowly in April air,
so almost-falling, so hinderingly
dangling from the neck of the movers' crane.
So on the edge of losing everything.

Let me teach like the first snow, falling.

2011

*An extraordinary evening in the garden, with such sweetness
and intensity of feeling. And the fact that it started raining, lightly,
and nobody moved—that just made it better.*
—Mark Doty

Poems selected by Brad Davis
Connecticut Poetry Circuit poem selected by Amy Russo
Fresh Voices poem selected by Mimi Madden

Featuring

Patricia Hale (winner, Sunken Garden Poetry Prize)

Tony Hoagland

Luisa Caycedo-Kimura (Connecticut Poetry Circuit,

Southern Connecticut State University)

Ekiwah Adler-Belendez

Elizabeth Thomas

Dick Allen

Carolyn Orosz (Fresh Voices, Greater Hartford Academy of the Arts)

Patricia Smith

David Watts (runner-up Sunken Garden Poetry Prize)

Mark Doty

Also read: Fresh Voices from Connecticut High Schools

Siarna Kinney, Bacon Academy

Terence Lee, Newtown High School

Danilo Machado, Westhill High School

Laura Salvatore, Bacon Academy

Connecticut Poetry Circuit

Kate Lund, Yale University

Tim Pettus, University of Hartford

Hannah Watkins, Middlesex Community College

Joseph Welch, University of Connecticut

The Facts

It was the boy who lived down the street,
my own brother's age but not like him—
tougher, quieter, more dangerous,
the kind of boy you knew had a blade
in his back pocket instead of a comb;
whose mother was so thin and faded
you couldn't even make out the print of her dress;
whose father packed his bags and moved
to Wheeling, West Virginia,
where he already had another wife,
another life, another pack of kids;
a boy who quit school and moved out at 17
to an apartment in the city where they said
he kept a skull on the mantle
and a stash in the top dresser drawer;
who a couple years later, when a cop asked
did he ever take a bath, stuck out his chin
and said he never took nothing;
the boy whose arrest photo I cut
from the Sunday Pittsburgh Press
and mounted in my blue leatherette album.
He was the one who saw me there
on the bottom of the pool, stunned
from a wild elbow to the head,
gazing around me calmly surprised
by the thought I might be drowning.
He was the one who grabbed my wrist,
pulled me to safety, then without a word,
went back to his friends on the other side,
leaving me breathless.

Romantic Moment

After seeing the nature documentary we walk down Canyon Road,
onto the plaza of art galleries and high end clothing stores

where the orange trees are fragrant in the summer night
and the pink adobe walls glow flesh-like in the dark.

It is just our second date, and we sit down on a bench,
holding hands, not looking at each other,

and if I were a bull penguin right now I would lean over
and vomit softly into the mouth of my beloved,

and if I were a peacock I'd flex my gluteal muscles to
erect and spread the quills of my Cinemax tail.

If she were a female walkingstick bug she might
insert her hypodermic proboscis delicately into my neck

and inject me with a rich hormonal sedative
before attaching her egg sac to my thoracic undercarriage,

and if I were a young chimpanzee I would break off a nearby treelimb
and smash all the windows in the plaza jewelry stores.

And if she was a Brazilian leopardfrog she would wrap her impressive
tongue three times around my right thigh and

pummel me lightly against the surface of our pond
and I would know her feelings were sincere.

Instead we sit awhile in silence, until
she remarks that in the relative context of tortoises and iguanas,

human males seem to be actually rather expressive.
And I say that female crocodiles really don't receive

enough credit for their gentleness.
Then she suggests that it is time for us to go

to get some ice cream cones and eat them.

LUISA CAYCEDO-KIMURA

Cattleya Trianae in the Church of a Seventh Grade Garden

At thirteen she dreams she could live
beside a turquoise moon and dance to maracas
and congas barefoot in rhythm-tamed snow.

But sun comes home to the projects like a rotten
orange. Far from the beat of mangos, tías, and guavas,
her soul-curling swatting of roaches begins.

She trudges to her new school with the yell
of the wind, where her olive skin will soon darken
the room and make faces quickly frown with her winter.

She knows the school courtyards would be less
lonely if she were a daisy whose eyes open
to the geometry of a suburban lawn. So she skips

the English test — she already knows the answers —
and hides her faith in the front of the church
wondering if a belfry is high enough to jump from.

This orchid wishes to fly in a box of lost painted wings.
She clings to the fence of the schoolyard and works
herself into a weed. She grows knowing with no name.

Love song to my motorized wheelchair

Though we are almost married
I often forget you

You're bulky and stout
I sit around you most of the time.
You're cranky and lumbering.

But then I turn you on

And I remember
I love you
on high speed
all cranked
up. I love you
recklessly
rolling with me
the joystick is yours
throbbing in full gear
as we bump
denting the floor —

Every night you wait
for me to charge you up

and you come squeaking
like an ungainly pigeon
asking for more.

If I don't please you right
your weight might
crush my bones

When you tie me down
I only soar higher.
Yet you love to see me wriggling
all bound up and when I try
to pull out you hold me in.

The women who fall for me
are often paralyzed by you

They are jealous of how
I'm always lap dancing on you.
We're almost sewn at the hip.

Oh my
dark dawn
Oh my loyal task master
Oh my electric
steel tempered mistress.

ELIZABETH THOMAS

My Muse

the spirit regarded as inspiring a poet
—Webster's Dictionary

When I call on my muse
she looks the other way—
out the window
under her desk
twirls a strand of purple hair
imagines me invisible.
Acts like no one stands
in front of the classroom
asking about the sound of the color red.

My muse would like to kick my ass.
He slouches hard
in the back row
arms crossed
eyes angry
doesn't have a pen
doesn't want to borrow mine
doesn't want to be there
but when the bell rings
at the end of the period
he takes his time
and when no one is looking
flips a tiny square of poetry
on the desk in front of me
and makes my day.

My muse flip flops yellow
down school hallways
wears lime green high-tops
with black fishnet stockings
I wish I had the nerve to wear.
He's also a sweet sixth grader
who smells like bubblegum
and empty apartments
sports blue braces
and a chipped front tooth
has mohawked hair
and droopy drawers
and it's all I can do
not grab hold and pull them up.

My muse sees the world
through funky glasses —
a world both starlit
and nightmare black.
A world he wants to push away.
A world he wants to cling to.
A world of phantom roller coasters

and he's not tall enough
to get on and ride
so he waits alone
behind the fence
and imagines what it's like to let go.
And when he doesn't have the answers
he just might look to poetry
for the words.

My muse is high maintenance —
a complex ballerina
a wanna-be thug.
When he says, "I can't write no poetry"
I say, "Good, so let's write some."
She says, "Poetry is a snoozefest."
I say, "Rise and shine!"
He says, "But Miss, it's hard to think."
I say, "Write that down.
It's a good line for a poem."
She wants to know
can she write about her best friend's brother
who got shot last week
the Daddy he ain't never seen
someone's mama fighting in Iraq
another mother lost to crack
a slamming door
the bathroom bully
the kid too skinny, too short, too smart.
And I weep at their rough edges
their skinned knees —
the exposed poetry
of their lives.

My muse talks shit like
"That poem was dope, was
ill, was wack!"
and I smile, nod my head and wonder
"Is that good

or bad?"
And when she really wants my attention
she says, "Yo, Miss!
Are you the poet?"
And every time this happens
I am again bloodied and reborn
and say, "Yes,
I am the poet —
When you and you
and all of you exist,
so do I."

DICK ALLEN

This Far

for my daughter

Here, I leave you. There are tins of water
enough to keep you for a little while,
dried meat and biscuits by the pantry door.
Usually, the mice stay pretty quiet.

The view's not bad. Those are my favorite hills,
covered with pines. On a clear April day
you can see small paths among the boulders,
maybe an eagle if you're looking hard.

Try to remember that the telephone
is only for emergencies — may they be few.
Keep the doorsill swept. You can never tell
who will come riding up from the valley.

These are my books, a motley varied lot,
some too much read, some not much read at all.
If you want, replace them with your own,
or use the shelves for toys and flower vases.

You're going to be on your own — sometimes
for months on end. I've found it helps
to whistle frequently or make out lists
of foods you love and states you've traveled in.

The pump is just outside. The clothesline holds
two weeks of laundry if you're planning things.
Fasten garbage lids on tight. Little devils
come from the woods to forage every night.

I hope you like the sound of mountain streams,
by my count three. But I suspect a fourth
is somewhere out there. Every spring
I think I hear it flowing through the dark.

You might listen for it, too. But now
I've said enough. It's yours. And don't forget
I've left you butter in the blue and silver dish
and stubs and stalks of candles you may light.

CAROLYN OROSZ

Obituary (or the things it should have said)

i went into the attic yesterday and i found your hands (at least the imprint of
them on things you'd held) i touched your Reeboks the ones worn down by
miles of concrete and asphalt and dirt the ones burnt in parts black like charcoal
[*faszenet*] hole in the bottom of the left one and i just thought i'd let you know
that they still smell like burning rubber the ones the nurse handed to us in a
ziploc along with your watch and your shirt which was also burnt but straight
down the middle and in the shape ironically of a lightning bolt

it matched the scar on your chest the one i saw when my mother lifted the
sheets away i traced it heated and electric i touched your body for the last time
before they cut you open stole parts of you that were still whole ladled them like
soup into the bodies of strangers [*idegennek*] i put your shoes back in the box

picked up your notebook empty except for 187 Hungarian words [*homár,*
elereszt, csilla] words in your fathers native tongue a language you longed to
speak to write poetry in a way you were sure your father would understand you
forgot the word daughter [*lány*] you only knew me twelve years and you didn't
even hold me, a jewel in your abdomen like my mother had i was such a small
part of your existence, if i was a part at all and i just wanted to tell you that i still
recognize your handwriting

PATRICIA SMITH

Why A Colored Girl Will Slice You if You Talk Wrong About Motown

The men and women who coupled, causing us, first
arrived confounded. Surrounded by teetering towers
of *no, not now* and *you shoulda known better,* they
cowered and built little boxes of northern home,
crammed themselves inside, feasted on the familiar
of fat skin and the unskimmed, made gods of doors.
When we came — the same insistent bloody and question
we would have been down south — they clutched us,
plumped us on government cereal drenched in Carnation,
slathered our hair, faces, our fat wiggling arms and legs
with Vaseline. We shined like the new things we were.
The city squared its teeth, smiled oil, smelled the sour
each hour left at the corner of our mouths. Our parents
threw darts at the day. They romanced shut factories,
waged hot battle with skittering roaches and vermin,
lumbered after hunches. Their newborn children grew
like streetlights. We grew like insurance payments.
We grew like resentment. And since no tall sweetgum
thrived to offer its shouldered shade, no front porch
lesson spun wide to craft our wrong or righteous,
our parents loosed us into the crumble, into the glass,
into the hips of a new city. They trusted exploded
summer hydrants, scarlet licorice whips and crumbling

rocks of government cheese to conjure a sort of joy,
trusted joy to school us in the woeful limits of jukeboxes
and moonwash. Freshly dunked in church water, slapped
away from double negatives and country ways, we were
orphans of the north star, dutifully sacrificed, our young
bodies arranged on sharp slabs of boulevard. We learned
what we needed, not from our parents and their rumored
south, but from the gospel seeping through the sad gap
in Mary Well's grin. Smokey slow-sketched pictures
of our husbands, their future skins flooded with white light,
their voices all remorse and atmospheric coo. Lil' Stevie
squeezed his eyes shut on the soul notes, replacing his
dark with ours. Diana was the bone our mamas coveted,
the flow of slip silver they knew was buried deep beneath
their rollicking heft. Every lyric, growled or sweet from
perfect brown throats, was instruction: *Sit pert, pout, and
seamed silk. Then watch him beg.* Every spun line was
consolation: *You're such a good girl. If he has not arrived,
he will.* Every wall of horn, every slick choreographed
swivel, threaded us with the rhythm of the mildly wild.
We slept with transistor radios, worked the two silver knobs,
one tiny ear bud blocking out the roar of our parents' tardy
attempts to retrieve us. Instead, we snuggled with the Temps,
lined up five pretty men across. And damned if they didn't
begin every one of their songs with the same word: *Girl.*

DAVID WATTS

winter

when the wind is murderous and the air
is cracking cold, you are the most beautiful.

a scientist would make a project out
of this. I'm just drawn to your lips.

Pescadero

The little goats like my mouth and fingers,

and one stands up against the wire fence, and taps on the fence-board
a hoof made blacker by the dirt of the field,

pushes her mouth forward to my mouth,
so that I can see the smallish squared seeds of her teeth, and the bristle-
whiskers,

and then she kisses me, though I know it doesn't mean "kiss,"

then leans her head way back, arcing her spine, goat yoga,
all pleasure and greeting and then good-natured indifference: She loves me,

she likes me a lot, she takes interest in me, she doesn't know me at all
or need to, having thus acknowledged me. Though I am all happiness,

since I have been welcomed by the field's small envoy, and the splayed hoof,
fragrant with soil, has rested on the fence-board beside my hand.

Chronology

The Sunken Garden Festivals and the Participants

	Poets	Musicians
Summer 1992		
June 10	Hugh Ogden	Teresa Kubiak
June 24	Sue Ellen Thompson	Louis Ramao
July 15	Charles Darling	Patricia Kenziorski
July 29	Marilyn Nelson	Lisa Eells
August 12	Pit Pinegar	Deby Pasternak
	Pam Nomura	
August 26	Emily Holcombe	
	Steve Foley	
September 9	Elizabeth Kincaid-Ehlers	
	David Holdt	
	Susan Gimignani Lukas	
	Rennie McQuilkin	
September 23	Rennie McQuilkin	
Summer 1993		
June 23	James Merrill	Juan Britos, Victor Clavijo
July 7	Carole Stasiowski	Paul Recker
July 21	Robert Cording	Bryan-Allison Duo
August 4	Norah Pollard	Louis Ramao, Robin Wroblewski
August 18	*Fresh Voices*	
Septmber 1	Bessy Reyna	
Summer 1994		
June 15	Richard Wilbur	Village Fair
June 29	Kate Rushin	Allen White
July 13	Honor Moore	Lou Ramao, Robin Wroblewski
July 27	Martín Espada	Tequila!
August 10	*Fresh Voices*	Hall High Jazz Sextet
August 24	Ted Deppe	Anhared Stowe

	Poets	Musicians

Summer 1995

June 7	Galway Kinnell	Janet Marlowe
June 21	Cheryl Savageau	Lee Mixashawn
July 5	Jeffrey Harrison	Farmington Valley Symphony Orchestra
July 19	Sue Ellen Thompson	Pat Werne, Joan Leo
August 2	Patricia Smith	Kunle Mwanga Jazz Quartet
August 16	*Fresh Voices*	Hall High Jazz Quartet
August 30	Donald Hall	Bryan-Allison Duo

Summer 1996

June 12	Stanley Kunitz	Rhonda Larson
June 26	Sharon Olds	Village Fair
July 10	Brendan Galvin	Peace Brothers
July 24	Marge Piercy	A Klez Act
August 7	*Fresh Voices*	Kent Hewitt/Tim Moran Duo
August 21	Marilyn Nelson	I Giovanni Solisti String Quartet

Summer 1997

June 11	Mark Doty	CT Natural Horn Ensemble
June 25	*Fresh Voices*	Tom Callinan, Tony Morris
July 9	Patricia Smith	Collective Expression Quintet
July 23	Dick Allen	Clark-Schuldman Duo
August 6	Naomi Ayala	Sirius Coyote
August 20	Billy Collins	Pan Seton Lorenzo

Summer 1998

June 10	Carolyn Forché	Rhonda Larson
June 24	Natasha Trethewey	Pan Caribé
July 8	Margaret Gibson	Kent Hewitt/Tim Moran Duo
July 22	Leo Connellan	Sally Rogers
August 5	*Fresh Voices*	Hall High Jazz Combo
August 18	Hayden Carruth	Hugh Blumenfeld Trio
September 2	Lucille Clifton	CONCORA (performed a suite, written by Gwyneth Walker during the Clifton reading)

	Poets	Musicians
Summer 1999		
June 9	Eamon Grennan	Tom Callinan, Ann Shapiro
June 23	Gray Jacobik	Marian Maccarone, Tim Stella
July 7	Stephen Dunn	The Atlantic Brass Quintet
July 21	Joy Harjo	Sirius Coyote
August 4	*Fresh Voices*	I Giovanni Solisti
August 18	Billy Collins	The Virtual Consort; Solarus
Summer 2000		
June 3	Philip Levine	Jazz Boulevard
June 17	Marie Howe	Paul Winter
July 5	Thomas Lux	A Klez Act
July 19	Susan Kinsolving	Serenata
August 2	*Fresh Voices*	Lily and Margreet Francis
	Andrew Drozd	
	Erica Kim	
	Stephanie Green	
	Zach Sussman	
	Adrian Kudler	
	Sakima Stringer	
	Scott Guild	
	Cailin Doyle	
August 16	Martín Espada	José González & Criollo Clásico
Summer 2001		
June 13	Sonia Sanchez	Sol Sin Fronteras
June 27	Rennie McQuilkin	Connecticut Opera
July 11	Linda McCarriston	Swivel Hips
July 25	Edgar Gabriel Silex	Anhared Stowe
August 8	*Fresh Voices*	*Young Musicians*
	Maggie Crowley	Maya Shankar
	Tarray Daniels	Jennifer Hsiao
	Cassandra Faustini	
	Chris Gyngell	
	Rebekah Hayes	
	Amy Ma	
	Emily Madsen	
August 22	Doug Anderson	Kurt Elling
	Peter Schmitt	

	Poets	Musicians

Summer 2002

June 12	Yusef Komunyakaa	Guy Davis
June 26	Vivian Shipley	Home Cookin'
July 10	Wesley McNair	Sue Terry Trio
July 24	Marilyn Chin	Connecticut Gay Men's Chorus
August 7	*Fresh Voices*	*Young Musicians*
	Catherine Adams-Besancon	Kathleen Mary Kan
	Yiyin Erin Chen	Yiyin Erin Chin
	Hannah Goldfield	
	Johanna Klotz	
	Laurel Mandelberg	
	Cindy Martinez	
	Jennifer Steele	
August 21	Steve Straight	Marqaux Hayes, Dave Giardina & Friends

Summer 2003

June 11	Maxine Kumin	Eight to the Bar
June 25	Jack Agüeros	Jose Gonzalez & Criollo Clasico
July 9	Margaret Gibson	Rhonda Larson
July 23	Tim Seibles	Vanessa Rubin
August 6	*Fresh Voices*	*Young Musicians*
	Ashley Coleman	Taylor Cowdery
	Hailey Gallant	Bonni Brodsky
	Laura Marris	
	Sarah Mikolowsky	
	Sarah Myers	
	Emily Steinert	
August 20	Tony Fusco	Eugene Friesen
	Wally Swist	

Summer 2004

June 2	Grace Paley	Val Ramos Flamenco Quartet
June 16	Richard Blanco	Kim Zombik Jazz Quartet
June 30	Suzanne Cleary	Deb Pasternak Band
July 14	Joan Joffe Hall	"Big Al" Wilson Band
July 28	Martha Collins	Taylor Cowdery

	Poets	Musicians
August 11	*Fresh Voices*	*Young Musicians*
	Emily Ayer	Maura Valenti
	Stephen Frechette	Emily Nagel
	Hannah Katch	
	Nicole Oliva	
	Eric Serrano	
	Jaclyn Sheltry	
August 25	Kate Rushin	Legacy: The Keepers of Tradition

Summer 2005

June 9	Gary Soto	Charles Flores Jazz Quintet
June 23	Edwina Trentham	Jeffrey Smith Jazz Quartet
July 7	Brad Davis	The Rivergods
	Douglas Goetsch	
July 21	Major Jackson	Arnold McCuller Band
August 4	*Fresh Voices*	*Young Musicians*
	Jessica Kim	Erica Anne MacArthur
	Lisa Kim	Sophie Bolton
	Molly LaFlesh	
	Tonya Malinowski	
	Maya Polan	
	Lily Press	
August 18	Cortney Davis	Maura Valenti

Summer 2006

June 8	Jane Hirshfield	Marta Gomez Quintet
June 22	Jim Daniels	Kim Zombik Jazz Quartet
July 6	Renée Ashley	The Joint Chiefs
	John Surowiecki	
July 20	Li-Young Lee	Stephen Haynes & Bugaboo
August 3	*Fresh Voices*	*Young Musicians*
	Charlotte Crowe	Philip Back
	Morgan Enowitch	Chelsea Knox
	Sarah Gardiner	
	Olivia Ho-Shing	
	Lauren Schwartzman	
August 17	Norah Pollard	Guy Davis

Summer 2007
A sabbatical year

Summer 2008

	Poets	Musicians
June 11	Robert Pinsky	Merge
June 25	Coleman Barks	Eugene Friesen
	Connecticut Poetry Circuit	
	Tess Bird	
	Lisa Butler	
	Chiara DiLello	
	Taylor Katz	
	Tyler Theofilos	
July 9	Billy Collins	Sheila Jordan & Cameron Brown
July 23	Patricia Fargnoli	Tessa Souter
	Ilya Kaminsky	
August 6	Paul Muldoon	Rackett
August 20	*Fresh Voices*	Freddie Bryant
	Britta Bell	
	Sasha Debevec-McKenney	
	Jameson Fitzpatrick	
	Hannah Loeb	
	Nicole Marella	

Summer 2009

	Poets	Musicians
June 10	Robert Hass	Classical Spirits
	Brenda Hillman	
June 24	Baron Wormser	Uptown Trio
	Connecticut Poetry Circuit	
	Matthew Gilbert	
	Jordan Jacks	
	Susanna Myserth	
	Sarah Nichols	
	Katie Rowe	
July 8	Kim Roberts	Freddie Bryant
	Fresh Voices	
	Charlotte Beach	
	Martina Crouch	
	Emily Delano	

	Poets	Musicians
	Melanie Lieberman	
	Alexander Guarco	
July 22	Marilyn Nelson	Tomas Doncker
	Cave Canem	
	Lita Hooper	
	Opal Palmer Adisa	
	Carleasa Coates	
	John Murillo	
August 5	C. K. Williams	The Bagboys
	Don Thompson	
Summer 2010		
June 9	Galway Kinnell	Chris Norman & Eamon O'Leary
June 23	Bessy Reyna	Common Ground
	Gabrielle Calvocoressi	
July 7	Jean Valentine	CONCORA On the Town!
	Ginny Lowe Connors	
	Kate Lebo	
July 21	Terrance Hayes	Nat Reeves Ensemble
	Connecticut Poetry Circuit	
	John Dudek	
	Caitlin Scott	
	Kristin Rocha	
August 4	Taylor Mali	Ed Fast with Conga Bop
	Fresh Voices	
	Megan Brookman	
	Elizabeth Nutt	
	Kerrylee Pelkey	
	Machael Stankiewicz	
	Victoria Chen	
	Andrew Bryce	
Summer 2011		
June 8	Tony Hoagland	Ol' Skool
	Pat Hale	
June 22	Ekiwah Adler-Belendez	Sirius Coyote
	Connecticut Poetry Circuit	
	Kate Lund	
	Joe Welch	

	Poets	Musicians
	Hannah Watkins	
	Tim Pettus	
	Luisa Cavedo-Kimura	
July 6	Dick Allen	Atwater-Donnelly Band
	Elizabeth Thomas	
July 20	Patricia Smith	Eric Bibb
	Fresh Voices	
	Siarna Kinney	
	Terence Lee	
	Danilo Machado	
	Carolyn Orosz	
	Laura Salvatore	
August 3	David Watts	Chris Casey Ensemble
	Mark Doty	

Contributors

EKIWAH ADLER-BELENDEZ is the author of five collections of poetry, the most recent being *Love on Wheels*. His life story and poetry was featured on NBC *Dateline*. He has given numerous talks, readings, and workshops in colleges, high schools, and festivals in Mexico and the United States. He has had the pleasure of reading with Li-Young Lee, Coleman Barks, Franz Wright, and Mary Oliver. His work is featured in blueflowerarts .com. His interests include performance, myth, disability studies, and mystical experience. He spends his time between Massachusetts and Mexico, where he was born and raised.

JACK AGÜEROS was born in East Harlem, New York City in 1934. A community activist who has written extensively on issues of immigration, Agüeros served as the Director of the Museo del Barrio in East Harlem for eight years. The recipient of numerous awards, he has published poetry, plays, and children's stories. As well, he has written works broadcast on television, and has a number of translations to his credit. Agüeros, diagnosed with Alzheimer's disease in 2004, lives in New York City.

DICK ALLEN was appointed Connecticut State Poet Laureate for 2010–2015. His books include the Zen Buddhism-influenced *Present Vanishing* (2009 Connecticut Poetry Book Award), *The Day Before: New Poems*, and *Ode to the Cold War: Poems New and Selected*. Allen has received a Pushcart Prize, N.E.A., and Ingram Merrill Poetry Writing Fellowships, among numerous other awards. Various collections of his poetry have been finalists for the National Book Critics Poetry Award, The PEN/Winship Award, and the Poetry Society of America's William Carlos Williams Award. Dick Allen's poems have been selected for *The Best American Poetry* volumes six times.

DOUG ANDERSON's most recent book is *Keep Your Head Down: Vietnam, the Sixties, and a Journey of Self Discovery*. He has poetry and prose forthcoming in the *Massachusetts Review*, *Cutthroat*, the *Cimarron Review*, and the *San Pedro River Review*. He lives in Providence, Rhode Island.

RENÉE ASHLEY is the author of three volumes of poetry: *Salt* (Brittingham Prize in Poetry), *The Various Reasons of Light*, and *The Revisionist's Dream*, as well as a novel, *Someplace Like This*, and two chapbooks, *The Museum of Lost Wings* and *The Verbs of Desiring*. She has received fellowships from the New Jersey State Council on the Arts in both poetry and prose and a poetry fellowship from the National Endowment for the Arts. She is on the faculty of Fairleigh Dickinson University's low-residency MFA Program in Creative Writing.

NAOMI AYALA has authored two books of poetry, *Wild Animals on the Moon* and *This Side of Early*. Her third, *Calling Home: Praise Songs and Incantations*, is forthcoming. She published a translation of Argentinean poet Luis Alberto Ambroggio's *The Wind's Archeology/La arqueología del viento*. She teaches at The Writer's Center (Bethesda, Maryland) and the Joiner Center for the Study of War and Social Consequences (UMASS-Boston). Recent work in Spanish appears in *Al pie de la Casa Blanca: Poetas hispanos de Washington, D.C.*

EMILY AYER was a student at Ledyard High School when she was selected to read at the festival.

COLEMAN BARKS' Rumi translations have sold two million copies worldwide. He collaborates with various Persian scholars to do this work, John Moyne, most notably. The most recent collection is *Rumi: The Big Red Book*. A collection of Coleman Barks' personal poetry is available in *Winter Sky: Selected Poems 1968–2008*. He taught American Poetry and Creative Writing at the University of Georgia. He is now retired. Two grown sons and four grandchildren live near him in Athens, Georgia.

RICHARD BLANCO's first book, *City of a Hundred Fires*, exploring his cultural identity as a Cuban-American, received the prestigious Agnes Starrett Poetry Prize from the University of Pittsburgh Press. His second book, *Directions to The Beach of the Dead*, won the 2006 PEN / American Beyond Margins Award for its continued exploration of the universal themes of place and homecoming. His poems have appeared in *The Best American Poetry 2000*, *Great American Prose Poems*, and have been featured on National Public Radio's *All Things Considered*. His third collection, *Looking for the Gulf Motel*, is forthcoming.

LARY BLOOM is the author of seven books, including *Letters from Nuremberg* (with Christopher J. Dodd), *The Test of Our Times* (with Tom Ridge), *Lary Bloom's Connecticut Notebook*, and *The Writer Within*. A former *New York Times* columnist, he writes monthly for *Connecticut Magazine*. He teaches in Fairfield University's MFA creative writing program, and with poet Suzanne Levine in their memoir workshops. He is also a playwright and lyricist, and, as founding editor of the *Hartford Courant*'s *Northeast* magazine, helped create the Sunken Garden Poetry Festival, Art For All, Connecticut Voices, and Mark Twain Days. For more, see www.larybloom.net.

GABRIELLE CALVOCORESSI is the author of *The Last Time I Saw Amelia Earhart* and *Apocalyptic Swing*, which was a finalist for The Los Angeles Times Book Award. She is the Poetry Editor of the *Los Angeles Review of Books*. She went to her first poetry readings at The Sunken Garden. She lives in Los Angeles.

HAYDEN CARRUTH authored numerous collections of poetry, including *Scrambled Eggs & Whiskey: Poems, 1991–1995*, for which he received the National Book Award. He was recipient of fellowships from the Bollingen Foundation, the Guggenheim Foundation, and the National Endowment for the Arts, and was honored with the Lenore Marshall Award, the Paterson Poetry Prize, the Vermont Governor's Medal, the Carl Sandburg Award, and the Ruth Lilly Prize, among many others. Also known for his works of criticism, Carruth taught for many years at Bucknell University and at the Graduate Creative Writing Program at Syracuse University.

LUISA CAYCEDO-KIMURA was born in Ibagué, Colombia, and grew up in New York City. Currently, she is a student at Southern Connecticut State University. She was selected a 2011 Connecticut Student Poet by the Connecticut Poetry Circuit. Her poems appear in *Folio*, *San Pedro River Review*, and *Connecticut Review*, and have also been included in writing curricula at colleges and universities.

VICTORIA CHEN was a student at O. E. Smith High School when she was selected to read at the festival.

MARILYN CHIN's books of poems include *Rhapsody in Plain Yellow*, *Dwarf Bamboo*, and *The Phoenix Gone, the Terrace Empty*. Her book of fiction is *Revenge of the Mooncake Vixen*. Born in Hong Kong, raised in Portland, Oregon, she teaches in the MFA program at San Diego State University and is on the mentor faculty of The City University of Hong Kong's low residency MFA program. She has won numerous awards, including the Radcliffe Institute Fellowship at Harvard, the Stegner Fellowship, and a Fulbright Fellowship to Taiwan. Her work is featured in many journals and anthologies.

SUZANNE CLEARY's poetry books are *Keeping Time* and *Trick Pear*. Winner of a Pushcart Prize, her poems have appeared in several anthologies including *Best American Poetry* and journals including *Atlantic Monthly*, *Poetry London*, and *Ploughshares*. She is professor of English at SUNY Rockland and also teaches in the Converse College low-residency MFA in Creative Writing program.

LUCILLE CLIFTON served as the Maryland Poet Laureate and a Chancellor of the Academy of American Poets. She authored many collections of poetry, including the Pulitzer Prize-nominated *Good Woman: Poems and a Memoir 1969–1980* and *Blessing the Boats: New and Selected Poems 1988–2000* (for which she received the National Book Award). She was also a prolific writer of children's books, and served as Distinguished Professor of Humanities at St. Mary's College of Maryland.

BILLY COLLINS's ninth collection of poems is *Horoscopes for the Dead*. He is the editor of *Poetry 180: A Turning Back to Poetry, 180 More: Extraordinary Poems for Everyday*, and *Bright Wings: An Illustrated Anthology of Bird Poems*. His poems have appeared in numerous publications including *The Best American Poetry* series. He is a Distinguished Professor at Lehman College, City University of New York, and a Distinguished Fellow of the Winter Park Institute at Rollins College.

MARTHA COLLINS is the author, most recently, of *White Papers* and the book-length poem *Blue Front*, which won an Anisfield-Wolf Award. Collins has also published four earlier collections of poems and two collections of co-translated Vietnamese poetry. Other awards include fellowships from the NEA, Bunting Institute, Witter Bynner Foundation, and Ingram Merrill Foundation, as well as three Pushcart Prizes and a Lannan Foundation residency fellowship. Pauline Delaney Professor of Creative Writing at Oberlin College until 2007, Collins served as Distinguished Visiting Writer at Cornell University in 2010, and is currently editor-at-large for *Field* magazine.

LEO CONNELLAN was born in Portland, Maine. Connellan won the Shelley Memorial Award from the Poetry Society of America and served as Connecticut's second Poet Laureate from 1996 until his death in 2001. He was poet-in-residence for the Connecticut State University System, and published thirteen collections of poetry, the most recent being *The Maine Poems*. His work is featured in anthologies such as *Poetry Like Bread* and *The Maine Poets: An Anthology of Verse*.

GINNY LOWE CONNORS is the author of the poetry collection *Barbarians in the Kitchen* and a chapbook *Under the Porch*, which won the 2010 Sunken Garden Poetry Prize. She has edited several poetry anthologies, including *Proposing on the Brooklyn Bridge* and *Essential Love*. The recipient of numerous poetry awards, Connors works as an English teacher in West Hartford, Connecticut.

ROBERT CORDING teaches at College of the Holy Cross where he is the Barrett Professor of Creative Writing. He has published six collections of poems: *Life-list* (Ohio State University Journal Award), *What Binds Us to This World*, *Heavy Grace*, *Against Consolation*, *Common Life*, and his newest, *Walking with Ruskin*. He has received two National Endowment for the Arts fellowships and two grants from the Connecticut Commission of the Arts. His poems have appeared widely.

MARTINA CROUCH was a student at Danbury High School when she was selected to read at the festival.

JIM DANIELS has published numerous books of poetry and short fiction, including, most recently, *Trigger Man*, *Having a Little Talk with Capital P Poetry*, and *From Milltown to Malltown*, a collaborative book with photographs. He has also written three independent films, most recently *Mr. Pleasant*. A native of Detroit, Daniels lives in Pittsburgh near the boyhood homes of Dan Marino and Andy Warhol.

CHARLES DARLING created the popular grammar website *Guide to Grammar & Writing* (cctc.commnet.edu/grammar/). For thirty-five years, he taught English at Capital Community College in Hartford, CT. His collections of poems are *The Saints of Diminished Capacity* and *The Man Who Could Freeze Time*.

BRAD DAVIS lives in Pomfret, Connecticut. Of his seven collections of poems, the most recent are *Opening King David* and *Self Portrait w/ Disposable Camera* (chapbook: finalist, Black Lawrence Press and White Eagle Coffee Store Press). Winner of an AWP Intro Journal Award and the Sunken Garden Poetry Prize (for the chapbook, *Short List of Wonders*), his poems have appeared in *Poetry*, the *Paris Review*, *Michigan Quarterly Review*, *Image*, *Puerto del Sol*, the *Connecticut Review*, *Ascent*, and elsewhere.

CORTNEY DAVIS, a nurse practitioner, is the author of *Details of Flesh*, *Leopold's Maneuvers*, and of three poetry chapbooks and two nonfiction collections, most recently *The Heart's Truth: Essays on the Art of Nursing*. Honors include the Prairie Schooner Poetry Book Prize, an NEA Poetry Fellowship, Connecticut Center for the Book Non-Fiction Prize, and three Connecticut Commission on the Arts Poetry Grants. Cortney is the poetry editor of *Alimentum: the Literature of Food*. For more see www.cortneydavis.com.

SASHA DEBEVEC-MCKENNEY was a student at Windsor High School when she was selected to read at the festival.

TED DEPPE worked as an R.N. for twenty years and now teaches in the Stonecoast MFA program in Ireland. He is the author of four books of poetry, *Children of the Air*, *The Wanderer King*, *Cape Clear*, and *Orpheus on the Red Line*. He has received two fellowships from the NEA and a Pushcart Prize. Deppe has served as writer-in-residence for Phillips Academy (Andover, Massachusetts), the Poet's House (Donegal, Ireland), and the James Merrill House (Stonington, Connecticut). Since 2000, he has lived in Ireland, where he directs Stonecoast in Ireland.

MARK DOTY's *Fire to Fire: New and Selected Poems*, won the National Book Award in 2008. He is the author of eight books of poems and four volumes of nonfiction prose. A professor at Rutgers University, he lives in New York City and on the east end of Long Island.

STEPHEN DUNN is the author of sixteen books of poetry, most recently *Here and Now*. His *Different Hours* won the 2001 Pulitzer Prize. He lives in Frostburg, Maryland.

MARTÍN ESPADA is the author of more than fifteen books. His latest collection of poems is *The Trouble Ball*. His previous collection, *The Republic of Poetry*, was a finalist for the Pulitzer Prize. The recipient of a Guggenheim Fellowship, a USA Simon Fellowship, and the National Hispanic Cultural Center Literary Award, Espada is a professor of English at the University of Massachusetts-Amherst.

PATRICIA FARGNOLI, New Hampshire Poet Laureate from 2006 to 2009, is the author of six collections of poetry. *Then, Something* won the ForeWord Silver Poetry Book Award and the Shelia Mooton Poetry Book Award. Her fifth collection, *Duties of the Spirit*, won the New Hampshire Jane Kenyon Literary Book Award for an Outstanding Book of Poetry. Her first book, *Necessary Light* was awarded the 1999 May Swenson Poetry Award. A Connecticut native now retired and living in Walpole, New Hampshire, she has published widely in journals and anthologies.

STEVE FOLEY's first full-length poetry collection is *A Place at the Table*. His chapbook is *With the Hollow of Your Hand*. He taught English in Connecticut public high schools for thirty-five years, retiring in 2007. A former winner of the New England Association of Teachers of English Poet of the Year award, Foley was named the recipient of the 2011–2012 Hugh Ogden Poetry Prize by Trinity College. He currently resides in Vero Beach, Florida, with his wife, Diane.

CAROLYN FORCHÉ is a poet, translator and editor of the ground-breaking anthology *Against Forgetting: Twentieth-Century Poetry of Witness*, collecting the work of poets who endured conditions of extremity during the past century. She has also published four award-winning books of poetry and three books of poetry in translation. Her poetry has been translated into over twenty languages, and she has given poetry readings throughout the United States and the world. She has taught poetry and literature for thirty-five years and is a professor at Georgetown University and the Director of the Lannan Center for Poetics and Social Practice.

TONY FUSCO is past editor of the *Connecticut River Review* and editor of *Caduceus*, poetry anthology of the Yale Medical Group. His work has appeared in the *Connecticut Review*, *Louisiana Literature*, the *Red Rock Review*, the *South Carolina Review*, the *Paterson Review*, *Chiron*, and others. He is the author of *Jessie's Garden*, *Droplines*, and three chapbooks. Awards include Sunken Garden Poetry Prize, Alan Ginsberg Poetry Contest, Joseph Brodine Contest, and Wallace W. Winchell Contest. He is president of the Connecticut Poetry Society and a member of the New England Poetry Club.

HAILEY GALLANT was a student at E. O. Smith High School when she was selected to read at the festival.

BRENDAN GALVIN is author of sixteen collections. *Habitat: New and Selected Poems 1965–2005* was a finalist for the National Book Award. His awards include a Guggenheim Fellowship, two NEA fellowships, the Sotheby Prize of the Arvon Foundation (England), *Poetry*'s Levinson Prize, and many others. He lives in Truro, Massachusetts.

MARGARET GIBSON has published ten books of poems, most recently *Second Nature*. Also *Long Walks in the Afternoon*, Lamont Selection; *Memories of the Future: the Daybooks of Tina Modotti*, co-winner, Melville Cane Award; *The Vigil*, finalist, National Book Award in Poetry; *Earth Elegy: New and Selected Poems*; *Icon and Evidence*; *Autumn Grasses*; *One Body*, 2008 Connecticut Book Award in Poetry. Her memoir, *The Prodigal Daughter*, was a finalist for the 2009 Connecticut Book Award in Memoir and Biography.

DOUGLAS GOETSCH is the author of three books of poems, most recently *Nameless Boy*, and the recipient of fellowships from the National Endowment for the Arts and the New York Foundation for the Arts. His work has been published in numerous journals and anthologies including the *New Yorker*, the *Gettysburg Review*, the *American Scholar*, *Best American Poetry*, and *The Pushcart Prize*. He is the founding editor of Jane Street Press.

EAMON GRENNAN's most recent book is *Out of Sight: New and Selected Poems*. Retired from Vassar College for some years, he teaches part-time in the creative writing department of Columbia University. Grennan divides his time between Poughkeepsie, New York, and the west of Ireland.

PAT HALE's work has appeared in *CALYX Journal, Sow's Ear, Long River Run, Dogwood, Connecticut River Review, Naugatuck River Review*, and other journals. Her awards include CALYX's 2005 Lois Cranston Memorial Poetry Prize, first prize in the 2007 Al Savard Poetry Competition, and the 2011 Sunken Garden Poetry Award. In 2009, she was a resident at Hedgebrook; her Sunken Garden chapbook, *Composition and Flight*, contains many of the poems written there. She is a long-time member of the poetry group, the PIPS, and serves on the board of directors for the Riverwood Poetry Series, Inc.

DONALD HALL was born in New Haven, Connecticut, in 1928. He graduated from Harvard and Oxford and taught at the University of Michigan until 1975, when he and his wife Jane Kenyon moved to Hall's family farmhouse in New Hampshire. Here, they both wrote poems, and Hall also wrote children's books, short stories, essays, memoir, and textbooks. In April of 1995, at age forty-seven, Jane died of leukemia.

JOAN JOFFE HALL learned to read, age 4, at the kitchen table while Mother's back was turned, and the next year showed the boy downstairs how to read. After further study at Vassar and Stanford, she taught for forty years, mostly at University of Connecticut, with a joint appointment in English and Women's Studies. Collections of poetry and prose — fiction and memoir — include *The Rift Zone* (finalist for the William Carlos Williams Prize), *Romance & Capitalism at the Movies* (nominated for a Pulitzer Prize), *In Angled Light*, and a volume of stories, *Summer Heat*.

JOY HARJO's seven books of poetry include *How We Became Human: New and Selected Poems*, and *She Had Some Horses*. Her awards include the New Mexico Governor's Award for Excellence in the Arts, a Rasmussen US Artists Fellowship, and the William Carlos Williams Award from the Poetry Society of America. She has released four albums of original music and won a NAMMY for Best Female Artist. Her one-woman show, *Wings of Night Sky, Wings of Light*, premiered in Los Angeles. Forthcoming is *Soul Talk, Song* from Wesleyan, and *Crazy Brave*, a memoir.

JEFFREY HARRISON is the author of four full-length books of poetry — most recently *Incomplete Knowledge* (runner-up for the 2008 Poets' Prize), and *The Names of Things*, selected poems published in England. A recipient of Guggenheim and NEA Fellowships, he has published poems in many magazines and anthologies and has taught at George Washington University, Phillips Academy, where he was the Roger Murray Writer-in-Residence, College of the Holy Cross, the Stonecoast MFA, Framingham State College, and the Frost Place in Franconia, New Hampshire. For more information: www .jeffreyharrisonpoet.com.

ROBERT HASS's most recent books are *The Apple Trees at Olema: Selected Poems* and *What Light Can Do: Essays 1985–2010*. Born in San Francisco, he teaches at the University of California at Berkeley. He has translated the Japanese haiku masters and co-translated the poetry of Czeslaw Milosz. His poems have received the National Book Critics Circle Award, the National Book Award, and the Pulitzer Prize.

TERRANCE HAYES is the author of four books of poetry, including *Lighthead*, which won the 2010 National Book Award. He lives and teaches in Pittsburgh, Pennsylvania.

BRENDA HILLMAN has published eight poetry collections from Wesleyan University Press: *White Dress, Fortress, Death Tractates, Bright Existence, Loose Sugar, Cascadia, Pieces of Air in the Epic,* and *Practical Water* (winner, LA Times Book Award for Poetry); and three chapbooks: *Coffee, 3 A.M., Autumn Sojourn,* and *The Firecage*. She edited an edition of Emily Dickinson's poems and, with Patricia Dienstfrey, co-edited *The Grand Permisson: New Writings on Poetics and Motherhood*. She co-translated Jeongrye Choi's *Instances*.

JANE HIRSHFIELD's newest poetry collection is *Come, Thief*. Earlier books include *After* and *Given Sugar, Given Salt* (a finalist for the National Book Critics Circle Award). Her poems appear in the *New Yorker, Atlantic, Times Literary Supplement, Poetry, Mc-Sweeney's, Orion,* and in six editions of *The Best American Poetry*. Her honors include fellowships from the Guggenheim and Rockefeller foundations, NEA, and Academy of American Poets.

TONY HOAGLAND has published four collections of poems, of which the latest are *Unincorporated Persons in the Late Honda Dynasty* and *What Narcissism Means to Me*. His recognitions include the Jackson Poetry Prize, O.B. Hardisson Award for teaching, James Laughlin Award, and Mark Twain Award for humor in American poetry, as well as fellowships from the NEA and the Guggenheim Foundation. His essays about poetry appear widely. He has published a book of craft essays titled *Real Sofistakashun*. He teaches in the writing program at the University of Houston and in the Warren Wilson MFA program.

EMILY HOLCOMBE was born in Hartford, CT, and early on was greatly influenced by Emily Dickinson. She wrote her first poetry in her head before learning to read, and was writing poetry from age seven. She continued through high school and college, where she met Hugh Ogden, teacher and then fellow-poet. She joined a poetry group with him. Now she focuses on helping other writers. As a writing consultant at Hartford Seminary, she supports people writing about religious issues. She also helps local authors with their books and articles.

DAVID HOLDT teaches Freshman Writing at the University of Hartford. He has taught History and Writing at independent schools including Hotchkiss, Germantown Friends, and Westledge. At Watkinson School in Hartford he was Director of the Writing Program. He has two degrees from Wesleyan University and one from Duke. A member of The River's Edge Poets for over twenty years, his poems have appeared in such publications as *Amelia, Chelsea, Blueline, Aethlon, Spitball, Northwoods Journal, Embers, Connecticut River Review*, and in several anthologies. He has published numerous essays and produced two plays.

LITA HOOPER is the co-editor of *44 on 44: 44 African American Writers on the 44th President of the United States* and author of two books, *Thunder in Her Voice: The Journal of Sojourner Truth* and *Art of Work: The Art and Life of Haki Madhubuti*. Her work has appeared in anthologies, magazines, and journals. She is the recipient of writing fellowships from Cave Canem, The Virginia Center for the Creative Arts, and The Center for Book Arts. Dr. Hooper is an associate professor of English at Georgia Perimeter College where she teaches Creative Writing and African American Literature online.

OLIVIA HO-SHING was a student at The Masters School when she was selected to read at the festival.

MARIE HOWE is the author of three books of poetry, the most recent being *The Kingdom of Ordinary Time*. She teaches at Sarah Lawrence College and lives in New York City.

MAJOR JACKSON has two poetry collections: *Hoops* (finalist, NAACP Image Award) and *Leaving Saturn* (winner, Cave Canem Poetry Prize, and finalist, National Book Critics Circle Award). A third volume, *Holding Company*, is forthcoming. He received a Whiting Writers' Award and was honored by the Pew Fellowship and the Witter Bynner Foundation. He was a creative arts fellow at the Radcliffe Institute for Advanced Study and the Jack Kerouac Writer-in-Residence at the University of Massachusetts–Lowell. He teaches at University of Vermont and the Bennington Writing Seminars. He is Poetry Editor of the *Harvard Review*.

GRAY JACOBIK's collections include *Brave Disguises* (AWP Poetry Prize), *The Surface of Last Scattering* (X. J. Kennedy Prize), *The Double Task* (Juniper Prize), and a memoir-in-verse, *Little Boy Blue*. Gray holds a Ph.D. in British and American Literature from Brandeis University and is a professor emeritus having retired from Eastern Connecticut State University. For almost three decades, Gray's poems have been published widely, and many have received prizes. She is also a painter. For more information about Gray's work, please visit her website: grayjacobik.com.

ILYA KAMINSKY was born in Odessa, former USSR and arrived in the United States in 1993, when his family was granted asylum by the American government. He is the author of *Dancing in Odessa*, which won the American Academy of Arts and Letters' Metcalf Award, Whiting Writers Award, Lannan Fellowship, and other honors. He is also the co-editor of *Ecco Anthology of International Poetry*.

ELIZABETH KINCAID-EHLERS came to Connecticut in 1979 as Visiting Writer-in-Residence at Trinity College. She liked living in Connecticut so much that, when the contract ended, she went back to school and retrained to become a psychotherapist. Since the early 1980s she has maintained a private practice in West Hartford, all the while continuing to write, give readings, and, occasionally, teach. Her publications include *Seasoning: Poems 2005–2009*, *Leaping and Looming: Collected Poems 1979–2004*, and a new collection, *How Do I Hate Thee? A Sampler of Poetic Rage Against Cancer*.

GALWAY KINNELL, former MacArthur Fellow and State Poet of Vermont, won the Pulitzer and the National Book Award in 1982. His books include *The Book of Nightmares*; *Mortal Acts, Mortal Words*; *The Past*; *Imperfect Thirst*; *A New Selected Poems*; and, mostly recently, *Strong Is Your Hold*. He has translated works by Yves Bonnefoy, Yvan Goll, François Villon, and Rainer Maria Rilke and edited *The Essential Whitman*. He taught at New York University and served as a chancellor of the Academy of American Poets. In 2010 he was given the Academy's Wallace Stevens Award. He lives in Sheffield, Vermont.

SUSAN KINSOLVING's books of poems are *The White Eyelash*, *Dailies & Rushes* (a finalist for the National Book Critics Circle Award), *Among Flowers*, and (forthcoming) *My Glass Eye*. She has taught poetry in the Bennington Writing Seminars, University of Connecticut, Southampton College, Chautauqua Institute, Willard-Cybulski Men's Prison, California Institute of the Arts, and The Hotchkiss School. As a librettist, she has had works performed with the Marin Symphony, Santa Rosa Symphony, Glimmerglass Opera, and The Baroque Choral Guild in New York, The Netherlands, Italy, and California. She has received poetry fellowships from Connecticut, New York, Illinois, France, Italy, Scotland, and Switzerland.

YUSEF KOMUNYAKAA is the author of numerous collections of poetry, including *Neon Vernacular: New and Selected Poems 1977–1989* (Wesleyan University Press), for which he received the Pulitzer Prize. Other honors include Creative Writing Fellowships from the National Endowment for the Arts, the Thomas Forcade Award, the Kingsly Tufts Poetry Award, and the William Faulkner Prize. Komunyakaa was elected a Chancellor of the Academy of American Poets in 1999, and is currently Distinguished Senior Poet at New York University's graduate creative writing program.

MAXINE KUMIN's seventeenth poetry collection, *Where I Live: New and Selected Poems 1990–2010*, won the Los Angeles Times book prize in 2011. Her awards include the Pulitzer and Ruth Lilly Poetry Prizes, the Aiken Taylor Award, the Poets' Prize, and the Harvard Arts and Robert Frost Medals. A former U.S. Poet Laureate, she and her husband live on a farm in central New Hampshire.

STANLEY KUNITZ was named the United States Poet Laureate in 1974 and 2000. His honors include the Bollingen Prize, a Ford Foundation grant, a Guggenheim Foundation fellowship, Harvard's Centennial Medal, the Levinson Prize, the Harriet Monroe Poetry Award, a senior fellowship from the National Endowment for the Arts, and the National Medal of the Arts. He published numerous collections of poetry, including

Selected Poems, 1928–1958, for which he received the Pulitzer Prize, and *Passing Through: The Later Poems, New and Selected*, which won the National Book Award.

KATE LEBO is a poet and pie maker from Seattle, where she attends the University of Washington's MFA program. Her poems appear in *Best New Poets 2011*, *Poetry Northwest*, *Bateau*, and *The Portland Review*, and she's the recipient of a Nelson Bentley Fellowship, a 4Culture grant, and a Soapstone residency. For more about Kate's zine, *A Commonplace Book of Pie*, and other tasty treats, visit Pie-Scream.com.

LI-YOUNG LEE is the author of four collections of poems (*Rose*, *The City in Which I Love You*, *Book of My Nights*, and *Behind My Eyes*). He runs a poetry workshop once a month in Chicago, where he lives with his wife and six sons.

PHILIP LEVINE, current U.S. Poet Laureate, was born in 1928 in Detroit of Russian-Jewish immigrants, educated at the public schools and the city university of Detroit, Wayne University. He studied poetry and poetry writing with Robert Lowell, John Berryman, and Yvor Winters. In 1958, he settled in Fresno and taught at Fresno State for twenty-two years. In the mid-1960s, he lived two years in Spain. His seventeenth collection is *News of the World*. His work has won many awards including two National Book Awards, the National Book Critics Award, and the Pulitzer in 1995. He now divides his time between Brooklyn and Fresno.

SUSAN GIMIGNANI LUKAS, after many years of being part of The River's Edge Poets, left Connecticut in 1998 to live in her beloved Manhattan where she teaches writing and English at The Allen-Stevenson School. Missing her dear friends and colleagues deeply, she joined a small writing group in the city with whom she has continued the endless project of rewriting, revising, and editing both poetry and short fiction. She has two daughters and two grandsons, all of whom enrich her life a thousand fold.

THOMAS LUX has two books forthcoming, one of nonfiction, one of poetry. He is Bourne Professor of Poetry at The Georgia Institute of Technology. He lives in Atlanta.

EMILY MADSEN was a student at Avon High School when she was selected to read at the festival.

TAYLOR MALI was one of the original poets to appear on the HBO series *Russell Simmons Presents Def Poetry*. The author of two collections of poetry, *What Learning Leaves* and *The Last Time As We Are*, his work has appeared in anthologies and other publications including *The Outlaw Bible of American Poetry*, *The Idiot's Guide to Slam Poetry*, and *Spoken Word Revolution*. He runs the Page Meets Stage reading series at the Bowery Poetry Club in New York City. For more information: www.taylormali.com.

LINDA MCCARRISTON is from Lynn, Massachusetts, and lives now in Gloucester. Two grown sons and two granddaughters live in New York City. She started teaching high school English in 1965, after graduating from Emmanuel College in Boston, and never didn't write. Since 1994, she has taught at the University of Alaska Anchorage in an MFA program that recently became low-residency, published three books of poems to critical notice, and received various grants and awards. Her poems have got her in trouble for their "incendiary" mind and "layered inversion of meaning(s)."

WESLEY MCNAIR is poet laureate of Maine and has authored or edited eighteen books, including poetry, essays, and anthologies. His most recent volume of verse is *Lovers of the Lost: New & Selected Poems*. His poetry has appeared in the *Best American Poetry*, the *Pushcart Prize* annual, the *Writer's Almanac*, NPR's *Weekend Edition*, and in sixty anthologies. He has held grants from the Fulbright and Guggenheim foundations, two from the NEA in creative writing, and two Rockefeller fellowships. Selected for a United States Artists Fellowship in 2006, Philip Levine called him "one of the great storytellers of contemporary poetry."

RENNIE MCQUILKIN taught at Phillips Academy and Miss Porter's School before co-founding the Sunken Garden Poetry Festival. His poetry has appeared in the *Atlantic Monthly*, *Poetry*, the *American Scholar*, the *Southern Review*, the *Yale Review*, and other publications. The author of ten poetry collections, he has received fellowships from the National Endowment for the Arts and the State of Connecticut. He has received the Connecticut Center for the Book's Lifetime Achievement Award and its annual poetry award, and is currently the publisher of Antrim House Books. He and his wife, the artist Sarah McQuilkin, live in Simsbury, Connecticut.

JAMES MERRILL served as a Chancellor of the Academy of American Poets from 1979 until 1995. His novel, *The (Diblos) Notebook*, was a finalist for the National Book Award in Fiction, and the following year his *Nights and Days* won the National Book Award in Poetry. His awards for poetry include the Bollingen Prize for *Braving the Elements*, the Pulitzer Prize for *Divine Comedies*, a second National Book Award for *Mirabell*, the National Book Critics Circle Award for *The Changing Light at Sandover*, and the first Bobbitt National Prize for Poetry from the Library of Congress for *The Inner Room*.

HONOR MOORE is the author of three collections of poems, *Red Shoes*, *Darling*, and *Memoir*, and two works of nonfiction, *The Bishop's Daughter* (shortlisted for the National Book Critics Circle Award), and *The White Blackbird* (a *New York Times* notable book). For the Library of America, she edited *Amy Lowell: Selected Poems* and *Poems from the Women's Movement*. She has won awards for her poetry from the National Endowment for the Arts and the Connecticut Commission for the Arts, and for nonfiction from the John Solomon Guggenheim Foundation.

PAUL MULDOON's main collections of poetry are *New Weather*, *Mules*, *Why Brownlee Left*, *Quoof*, *Meeting the British*, *Madoc: A Mystery*, *The Annals of Chile*, *Hay*, *Poems 1968–1998*, *Moy Sand and Gravel*, *Horse Latitudes*, and *Maggot*. He writes lyrics for the Princeton-based music collective Wayside Shrines.

SUSANNA MYRSETH is from San Francisco. While at Wesleyan University she won the Sophie Reed Prize for Poetry.

MARILYN NELSON's books include *The Homeplace, Carver: A Life In Poems, Fortune's Bones, The Freedom Business*, and *A Wreath For Emmett Till*. Her honors include two fellowships from the N.E.A., a Guggenheim fellowship, three National Book Award Finalist medals, the Poets' Prize, the Boston Globe/Hornbook Award, a Newbery Honor medal, the Flora Stieglitz Straus Award, the Lion and Unicorn Award for Excellence in Poetry for Young Adults, the American Scandinavian Foundation Translation Award, and three honorary doctorates. Nelson is an emeritus professor at the University of Connecticut, the former Poet Laureate of Connecticut, and founder/director of Soul Mountain Retreat.

PAM NOMURA has chaired the Creative Writing programs at the Greater Hartford Academy of the Arts and the Center for Creative Youth at Wesleyan University. She has also served as director of the Poetry Center and Poetry-in-the-Schools Program at Trinity College. Pam has been in residence at Soul Mountain, the Blue Mountain Center, and most recently, in Cape Town, South Africa, where she partnered with South African artists to work with youth-at-risk. Her book of poems, *Water and Land by Turns*, was published by Hill-Stead Museum for the tenth anniversary celebration of the Sunken Garden Poetry Festival.

HUGH OGDEN taught for four decades at Trinity College in Hartford, Connecticut, where, in 1968, he co-founded the College's creative writing program. His last collection of poems was *Turtle Island Tree Psalms*. Ogden received a National Endowment for the Arts grant and two Connecticut Commission on the Arts Fellowships.

SHARON OLDS is the author of nine books of poetry, including *The Dead and the Living* (winner of the National Book Critics Circle Award), *The Unswept Room* (finalist for the National Book Award and the National Book Critics Circle), and *One Secret Thing* (a finalist for the Forward Prize). She is a Chancellor of the Academy of American Poets and teaches graduate poetry workshops at New York University.

CAROLYN OROSZ was a student at the Greater Hartford Academy of the Arts when she was selected to read at the festival.

GRACE PALEY was a writer of both fiction and poetry, and a Professor at Sarah Lawrence College for over twenty years. Her honors included the Guggenheim Fellowship, the Edith Wharton Award, and the Jewish Cultural Achievement Award in the Literary Arts. In 1989, New York Governor Mario Cuomo deemed her the first official New York State Writer. She served as Vermont State Poet Laureate from 2003 until 2007.

MARGE PIERCY's eighteenth poetry book, *The Hunger Moon: New & Selected Poems 1980–2010*, came out last spring. Her other books include *The Crooked Inheritance, The*

Moon Is Always Female, What Are Big Girls Made Of, with several in paperback. Piercy has published seventeen novels, recently *Sex Wars*; two early novels, *Dance the Eagle to Sleep* and *Vida*, have just been republished with new introductions. Her memoir is *Sleeping With Cats*. Her work has been translated into nineteen languages. She gives numerous readings, workshops, and occasional speeches here and abroad.

PIT MENOUSEK PINEGAR is the author of three books of poetry, *Nine Years between Two Poems, The Possibilities of Empty Space,* and *The Physics of Transmigration*. She also writes fiction, nonfiction, and plays. Her essays have been published in the *Chicago Tribune, Hartford Courant,* and *Saudi Gazette*. She is also a photographer, with a special interest in candid portraits of artists and writers. She has been nominated for a Pushcart Prize six times and has received the Governor's Distinguished Advocate of the Arts Award, as well as an artist fellowship from the Connecticut Commission on Culture and Tourism.

ROBERT PINSKY's *Selected Poems* was recently published. He edited *Essential Pleasures*, an anthology with accompanying audio CD. His honors include the Harold Washington Award from the city of Chicago, the *Los Angeles Times* Book Prize for his translation *The Inferno of Dante*, and the PEN-Volcker Award. For videos from the Favorite Poem Project, an organization that he founded during his tenure as U.S. Poet Laureate, visit www.favoritepoem.org.

NORAH POLLARD, in her grown-up years, worked as a secretary for Type-A bosses in steel and metal deposition, advertising, software engineering companies, and law firms. She's managed to keep her spirit afloat and her muse happy by visiting her river every evening—the nearby Housatonic, in Stratford, Connecticut—where she goes to get her sanity back.

LILY PRESS was a student at Danbury High School when she was selected to read at the festival.

BESSY REYNA is an award-winning poet whose works include the bilingual poetry book *Memoirs of the Unfaithful Lover/Memorias de la Amante Infiel*; the chapbooks *The Battlefield of Your Body* (Hill Stead Museum), *She Remembers, Terrarium* (in Spanish); and a collection of short stories *Ab Ovo* (in Spanish). She was a frequent contributor to *Northeast*, the Sunday magazine of the *Hartford Courant* where she also worked as an opinion columnist for several years. She edits the arts section for *Identidad Latina*, a Hartford-based Spanish language newspaper. For more, see www.bessyreyna.com.

KIM ROBERTS is the author of five books, most recently *Animal Magnetism* (winner of the 2011 Pearl Poetry Prize) and the anthology *Full Moon on K Street: Poems About Washington, DC*. Poems of hers have appeared in journals beginning with every letter of the alphabet, and have been translated into Spanish, Portuguese, German, and Mandarin. She has been a writer-in-residence at thirteen artist colonies. Roberts edits the online journal *Beltway Poetry Quarterly* and lives in Washington, D.C. Her website is www.kimroberts.org.

KRISTIN ROCHA is a previously unpublished poet from Providence, Rhode Island. She currently works in fashion publicity while living in Brooklyn, New York, but plans to pursue an MFA in poetry in the near future. Kristin is inspired by cities, bodies, and Spanish poets and counts the poets of the Women's Movement as some of her most important influences.

KATE RUSHIN is the author of *The Black Back-Ups*. A Grolier Poetry Prize winner, she received fellowships from Massachusetts Artists' Foundation, Cave Canem, and Fine Arts Work Center in Provincetown. She has taught at MIT, Brown, and Wesleyan where she directed their Center for African American Studies. Rushin was commissioned to write poems for the Connecticut Freedom Trail Poetry Project through the 2011 International Festival of Arts and Ideas and The African American Studies Department at Yale. A 1997 Connecticut Circuit Poet, she has served as a judge for Connecticut Young Writers.

SONIA SANCHEZ's books of poems include *Shake Loose My Skin: New and Selected Poems*, *Does Your House Have Lions?* (nominated for both the NAACP Image and National Book Critics Circle Awards), and *Homegirls & Handgrenades* (winner, American Book Award from the Before Columbus Foundation). She has also published numerous children's books and plays. Among many honors she has received the Peace and Freedom Award from Women International League for Peace and Freedom, Pennsylvania Governor's Award for Excellence in the Humanities, National Endowment for the Arts Award, and Pew Fellowship in the Arts. She taught English at Temple University until 1999.

CHERYL SAVAGEAU's most recent book of poetry is *Mother/Land*. She has received Fellowships in Poetry from the National Endowment for the Arts and the Massachusetts Artists Foundation. Her second book of poetry, *Dirt Road Home*, was a finalist for the Paterson Poetry Prize. Her quilts, paintings, poetry, and assemblage work were part of the Twisted Path Exhibit at the Abbe Museum in Bar Harbor, Maine.

PETER SCHMITT is the author of five poetry collections: *Renewing the Vows*, *Hazard Duty*, *Country Airport*, and two chapbooks, *Incident in an Apartment Complex: A Suite of Voices* and *To Disappear*. He has received The Lavan Award from The Academy of American Poets; The "Discovery"/*The Nation Prize*; is a two-time recipient of grants from The Florida Arts Council; and was awarded a Fellowship from The Ingram Merrill Foundation. His poems have been featured several times on National Public Radio's *Writers Almanac* (read by Garrison Keillor). He has taught creative writing and literature at The University of Miami since 1986.

TIM SEIBLES' books of poems include *Hurdy-Gurdy*, *Hammerlock*, and *Buffalo Head Solos*. He has received fellowships from the NEA and Provincetown Fine Arts Work

Center and an Open Voice Award from the 63rd Street Y in New York City. He has been a workshop leader for the Cave Canem Writers Retreat and for the Zora Neale Hurston/Richard Wright Foundation. Tim is visiting faculty for the University of Southern Maine's low-residential Stonecoast MFA and associate professor in Old Dominion University's English Department and MFA in writing. His work has been featured in many journals and anthologies.

VIVIAN SHIPLEY (Connecticut State University Distinguished Professor and Editor of *Connecticut Review*) teaches at Southern Connecticut State University. Her eighth book of poetry is *All of Your Messages Have Been Erased*. Nominated for the Pulitzer Prize, it won the 2011 Paterson Award for Sustained Literary Achievement and the Connecticut Press Club Prize for Best Creative Writing. Her sixth chapbook is *Greatest Hits: 1974–2010*. She was awarded a Connecticut Arts Grant for Poetry in 2011. She lives in North Haven, Connecticut, with her husband, Ed Harris.

EDGAR GABRIEL SILEX is the author of two poetry collections and has received fellowships from the National Endowment for the Arts and the Maryland State Arts Council. He lives in Laurel, Maryland.

PATRICIA SMITH's books include *Blood Dazzler* (a finalist for the 2008 National Book Award), *Teahouse of the Almighty* (a National Poetry Series selection), and the just-released *Shoulda Been Jimi Savannah*. Her work has appeared or is forthcoming in *Poetry*, the *Paris Review*, *TriQuarterly*, and in *Best American Poetry 2011* and *Best American Essays 2011*. She is a professor at the College of Staten Island, and she teaches for Cave Canem and in the low-residency MFA program at Sierra Nevada College.

GARY SOTO is the author of forty books for adults, young adults, and children. His best-known works include *Buried Onions*, *Living up the Street*, *A Summer Life*, *Baseball in April*, and *New and Selected Poems*. The Gary Soto Literary Museum is housed at Fresno City College.

CAROLE STASIOWSKI's poems have been published in *Spoon River Poetry Review*, *Northeast Magazine*, *Zone 3*, and other literary journals. While living in Connecticut, she was editor and poetry editor for the *Connecticut Writer* and helped to produce a series of poetry vignettes for Connecticut Public Television. She is a frequent participant at The Frost Place seminar and twenty-plus-years member of the Wood Thrush Poets. She has worked in hospital public relations and marketing for nearly thirty years and now lives with her son on Cape Cod.

JENNIFER STEELE was a student at Middletown High School when she was selected to read at the festival.

STEVE STRAIGHT is professor of English and director of the poetry program at Manchester Community College. His two books are *The Water Carrier* and *The Almanac*.

For many years Straight directed the Connecticut Poetry Circuit and ran the Seminar Series for the Sunken Garden Poetry Festival. He has given workshops on writing and teaching throughout the eastern United States and in Ireland. In 1998 he was named a Distinguished Advocate for the Arts by the Connecticut Commission on the Arts.

JOHN SUROWIECKI has authored three poetry books, *Barney and Gienka*, *The Hat City after Men Stopped Wearing Hats*, and *Watching Cartoons before Attending a Funeral*, and five chapbooks. *Mr. Z., Mrs. Z., J.Z., S.Z.*, is scheduled for publication. John recently won the Poetry Foundation Pegasus Award for verse drama, *Nimrod's* Pablo Neruda Prize, and a poetry fellowship from the State of Connecticut. His poetry has appeared in many publications including *Alaska Quarterly Review, Folio, Cider Press Review, Poetry, Prairie Schooner, Redivider, Rhino, West Branch, Wisconsin Review, Gargoyle, Margie,* and *Mississippi Review.*

ZACH SUSSMAN was a student at Weston High School when he was selected to read at the festival.

WALLY SWIST's most recent book, *Huang Po and the Dimensions of Love*, was chosen by Yusef Komunyakaa as a co-winner in the Crab Orchard Series Open Poetry Competition. His previous book, *Luminous Dream*, was chosen as a finalist in the 2010 FutureCycle Poetry Book Award. He has also published a scholarly monograph, *The Friendship of Two New England Poets, Robert Frost and Robert Francis.*

TYLER THEOFILOS is an Ohio native who graduated from Yale University in 2008. He is currently working toward an MFA in screenwriting at UCLA. Tyler's poetry has been published in the *Connecticut Review*, the *Yale Literary Magazine*, and Cornell University's *Rainy Day.*

ELIZABETH THOMAS is a published poet, performer, and educator. The author of three books of poetry, she reads her work throughout the United States, and in 2009 presented *Poetry as Theater* at the United Arab Emirates University in Dubai. Her time is devoted to designing and teaching writing programs to promote literacy and the power of written and spoken word. An advocate of youth in the arts, she is coach and organizer with Brave New Voices: International Youth Poetry Slam and Festival. Thomas believes poetry is meant to be heard out loud and in person. For more see www.upwordspoetry.com.

DON THOMPSON has been publishing since the early sixties, including a half-dozen chapbooks. Recently retired, he and his wife live on her family cotton farm in the southern San Joaquin Valley, the area where Don was born, has lived most of his life, and of which he has written more than anything else.

SUE ELLEN THOMPSON is the author of four books, most recently *The Golden Hour*, and the editor of *The Autumn House Anthology of Contemporary American Poetry*. Her work has been included in the *Best American Poetry* series, read on National Public

Radio by Garrison Keillor, and featured in former U.S. Poet Laureate Ted Kooser's nationally syndicated newspaper column. A two-time Pulitzer nominee, she has taught at Middlebury College, Binghamton University, Central Connecticut State University, and The Writer's Center in Bethesda, Maryland. A long-time resident of Connecticut, she moved to Maryland's Eastern Shore in 2006 and was awarded the 2010 Maryland Author Award.

EDWINA TRENTHAM is a professor of English at Asnuntuck Community College, where she edits *Freshwater*, a national poetry journal. She has published poems in *Prairie Schooner*, *Massachusetts Review*, *Connecticut Review*, and *American Scholar*. Her first collection of poetry was *Stumbling into the Light*. She was awarded a 2010 Solo Writers Fellowship by the Greater Hartford Arts Council and the Beatrice Fox Auerbach Foundation Fund at the Hartford Foundation for Public Giving. She lives in Moodus, Connecticut, with her husband, Greg Coleman, a poet, labyrinth designer, and Tai Chi Instructor.

NATASHA TRETHEWEY is author of *Beyond Katrina: A Meditation on the Mississippi Gulf Coast*, and three collections of poetry, *Domestic Work*, *Bellocq's Ophelia*, and *Native Guard* (for which she was awarded the Pulitzer Prize). She is the recipient of NEA, Guggenheim, Bunting, and Rockefeller fellowships. At Emory University she is professor of English and holds the Phillis Wheatley Distinguished Chair in Poetry.

JEAN VALENTINE's first book *Dream Barker* was chosen for the Yale Series of Younger Poets. Her most recent collection is *Break the Glass*. Valentine has been awarded grants and fellowships from the Rockefeller Foundation, the National Endowment for the Arts, the Guggenheim Foundation, and the Bunting Institute. In 2000, she received the Shelley Memorial Prize from the Poetry Society of America, and in 2009 the Wallace Stevens Award from the Academy of American Poets. Valentine taught at New York University until 2004, and currently lives in New York City.

DAVID WATTS has published seven books of poetry (two under the pseudonym, harvey ellis), two books of nonfiction short stories, and a CD of Word-Jazz. He is an NPR commentator on *All Things Considered*, producer of the PBS documentary *Healing Words: Poetry and Medicine*, and a classically trained musician. He founded two summer workshops for poets and writers with an interest in illness and healing held at Sarah Lawrence College and Dominican University of California. He lectures on humanism in the healing arts at medical and nursing schools across the country.

RICHARD WILBUR's poetry collections include *Things of This World*, for which he received the Pulitzer Prize and the National Book Award, and most recently, *Anterooms: New Poems and Translations*. His honors include the Wallace Stevens Award, the Frost Medal, the Gold Medal for Poetry from the American Academy of Arts and Letters, the T. S. Eliot Award, two Guggenheim Fellowships, two PEN translation awards, and the Shelley Memorial Award. He was elected a chevalier of the Ordre des Palmes Aca-démiques and served as Poet Laureate of the United States, 1987–1988.

C. K. WILLIAMS' most recent books are *Wait* (poems) and *On Whitman* (essays). In addition to his *Collected Poems*, he has published nine other books of poetry. *The Singing* won the National Book Award for 2003; *Repair* was awarded the 2000 Pulitzer Prize; and an earlier work, *Flesh and Blood*, won the National Book Critics Circle Award. He teaches in the Creative Writing Program at Princeton University, and is a member of the American Academy of Arts and Letters.

BARON WORMSER is the author/co-author of twelve books including *The Road Washes Out in Spring: A Poet's Memoir of Living Off the Grid*; *Scattered Chapters: New and Se-lected Poems*; and *The Poetry Life: Ten Stories*. He directs the Frost Place Conference on Poetry and Teaching and teaches in the Fairfield University MFA Program.

Acknowledgments

Ekiwah Adler-Belendez: "Love Song to My Motorized Wheelchair" is used with the author's permission.

Jack Agüeros: "Psalm for Distribution" from *Lord, Is This a Psalm?* (Hanging Loose, 2002) by Jack Agüeros, is reprinted by permission of Hanging Loose Press.

Dick Allen: "Backstroking at Thrushwood Lake" from *Ode to the Cold War: Poems New and Selected.* Copyright © 1997 by Dick Allen. Reprinted with permission of The Permissions Company, Inc., on behalf of Sarabande Books, www.sarabandebooks .org. "This Far" from *The Day Before: New Poems.* Copyright © 2003 by Dick Allen. Reprinted with permission of The Permissions Company, Inc., on behalf of Sarabande Books, www.sarabandebooks.org.

Doug Anderson: "Blues" from *The Moon Reflected Fire* (Alice James, 2002) is used with the author's permission.

Renée Ashley: "What She Wanted" from *The Revisionist's Dream* (Avocet, 2001) is used with the author's permission.

Naomi Ayala: "El Placer de la Palabra" from *Wild Animals on the Moon and Other Poems* (Willimantic: Curbstone Press, 1997). Reprinted with permission of Northwestern University Press.

Emily Ayer: "Sacrilege" is used with permission from Hill-Stead Museum.

Coleman Barks: "What Was Said to the Rose," by Jalaluddin Rumi, translation © 2005 by Coleman Barks. Reprinted with the translator's permission.

Richard Blanco: "Winter of the Volcanoes: Guatemala" from *Directions to the Beach of the Dead* (University of Arizona Press, 2005). Copyright © 2005 by Richard Blanco. First published in "Puerto del Sol." Reprinted by permission of Stuart Bernstein Representation for Artists, New York. All rights reserved.

Gabrielle Calvocoressi: "Every Person in this Town Loves Football" is used with the author's permission.

Hayden Carruth: "Scrambled Eggs and Whiskey" from *Scrambled Eggs & Whiskey.* Copyright © 1996 by Hayden Carruth. Reprinted with permission of The Permissions Company, Inc., on behalf of Copper Canyon Press, www.coppercanyonpress.org.

Luisa Caycedo-Kimura: "Cattleya Trianae in the Church of a Seventh Grade Garden" first appeared in *San Pedro River Review* (spring 2011) and is used with the author's permission.

Victoria Chen: "Barbie Gone Conservative" is used with permission from Hill-Stead Museum.

Marilyn Chin: "25 Haiku" is used with the author's permission.

Suzanne Cleary: "Anyways" from *Trick Pear.* Originally published in *Southern*

Poetry Review (spring/summer 2003). Copyright © 2003, 2007 by Suzanne Cleary. Reprinted with permission of The Permissions Company, Inc., on behalf of Carnegie Mellon University Press, www.cmu.edu/universitypress.

Lucille Clifton: "the thirty eighth year" from *The Collected Poems of Lucille Clifton*. Copyright © 1969 and 1987 by Lucille Clifton. Reprinted with permission of The Permissions Company, Inc., on behalf of BOA Editions, Ltd, www.boaeditions.org.

Billy Collins: "Japan" and "The Death of the Hat" from *Picnic, Lightning*, by Billy Collins, © 1998. Reprinted by permission of the University of Pittsburgh Press. "The Lanyard," copyright © 2005 by Billy Collins, from *The Trouble with Poetry* by Billy Collins. Used by permission of Random House, Inc.

Martha Collins: "Field" is used with the author's permission.

Leo Connellan: "Shooter" from *Provincetown* (Willimantic: Curbstone Press, 1995) is used with permission of Northwestern University Press.

Ginny Lowe Connors: "Under the Porch" is used with the author's permission.

Robert Cording: "Kafka: Lilacs" from *What Binds Us to This World* (Copper Beech) is reprinted with the author's permission.

Martina Crouch: "Summersick" is used with permission from Hill-Stead Museum.

Jim Daniels: "You bring out the boring white guy in me" from *Revolt of the Crash-Test Dummies* (Eastern Washington University Press). Reprinted by permission of the author.

Charles Darling: "In Certain Lights" is used with permission from the family of Charles Darling.

Brad Davis: "Common as Air" from *Opening King David* (Resource Publications, 2011). First appeared in *Image*. Used by permission of Wipf and Stock Publishers, www.wipfandstock.com.

Cortney Davis: "Nunc Tu Alma" reprinted from *Leopold's Maneuvers* by Cortney Davis by permission of the University of Nebraska Press. Copyright 2004 by the Board of Regents of the University of Nebraska.

Sasha Debevec-McKenney: "what i left on capen street" is used with permission of Hill-Stead Museum.

Ted Deppe: "The Book of God" is reprinted with the author's permission.

Mark Doty: "Pescadero" first appeared in the *New Yorker*. Used with author's permission. "Visitation" from *Sweet Machine* by Mark Doty. Copyright © 1998 by Mark Doty. Reprinted by permission HarperCollins Publishers and used also by permission of Random House, UK.

Stephen Dunn: "Imagining Myself My Father" from *Loosestrife* by Stephen Dunn. Copyright © 1996 by Stephen Dunn. Used by permission of W. W. Norton & Company, Inc.

Martín Espada: "The Other Alamo" and "*Preciosa* Like a Last Cup of Coffee" are reprinted with the author's permission.

Patricia Fargnoli: "Duties of the Spirit" from *Duties of the Spirit*, published by Tupelo Press. Copyright © 2005, Patricia Fargnoli. Used with permission.

Steve Foley: "Angel" is reprinted with the author's permission.

Carolyn Forché: "Curfew" from *Blue Hour* by Carolyn Forché. Copyright © 2003 by Carolyn Forché. Reprinted by permission of HarperCollins Publishers.

Tony Fusco: "The Litany of Streets" was first published in *The South Carolina Review*. Used with author's permission.

Hailey Gallant: "Roots" is used with the author's permission.

Brendan Galvin: "For a Little Girl of Pompeii" from *Great Blue: New and Selected Poems* (University of Illinois Press, 1990). Reprinted with author's permission.

Margaret Gibson: "Prayer Ascending, Prayer Descending" from *Earth Elegy* (LSU Press) and "Strange Altars" from *Icon and Evidence* (LSU Press) are reprinted with permission from Louisiana State University Press.

Douglas Goetsch: "Sofa-Bed" is reprinted with permission from Cleveland State University Poetry Center.

Eamon Grennan: "Wing Road" from *Relations: New & Selected Poems*. Copyright © 1998 by Eamon Grennan. Reprinted with permission of The Permission Company, Inc., on behalf of Graywolf Press, Minneapolis, Minnesota, www.graywolfpress.org. "Wing Road" from *Selected and New Poems* (2000) reprinted by kind permission of the author and The Gallery Press, www.gallerypress.com.

Pat Hale: "The Facts" is reprinted with the author's permission.

Donald Hall: "Without" from *Without: Poems* by Donald Hall. Copyright © 1998 by Donald Hall. Reprinted by permission of Houghton Mifflin Harcourt Publishing Company. All rights reserved.

Joan Joffe Hall: "Seed Sack" is reprinted with the author's permission.

Joy Harjo: "The Path to the Milky Way Leads Through Los Angeles" from *A Map to the Next World: Poems and Tales* by Joy Harjo. Copyright © 2000 by Joy Harjo. Used by permission of W. W. Norton & Company, Inc.

Jeffrey Harrison: "Totem," from *The Names of Things: New and Selected Poems*. Copyright © 2006 by Jeffrey Harrison. Used by permission of The Waywiser Press, Chipping Norton, England.

Robert Hass: "August Notebook: A Death" (section 4) from *The Apple Trees at Olema* by Robert Hass. Copyright © 2010 by Robert Hass. Reprinted by permission of HarperCollins Publishers.

Terrance Hayes: "Cocktails with Orpheus" from *Lighthead* by Terrance Hayes, copyright © 2010 by Terrance Hayes. Used by permission of Penguin, a division of Penguin Group (USA) Inc.

Brenda Hillman: "The Late Cold War" from *Practical Water* © 2009 by Brenda Hillman. Reprinted by permission of Wesleyan University Press.

Jane Hirshfield: "The Bell Zygmunt" from *After: Poems* by Jane Hirshfield.

Philip Levine: "Among Children" from *What Work Is* by Philip Levine. Copyright © 1991 by Philip Levine. Used by Permission of Alfred A. Knopf, a division of Random House, Inc.

Susan Gimignani Lukas: "Spring Cleaning at Night" is used with the author's permission.

Thomas Lux: "Refrigerator, 1957" is reprinted with the author's permission.

Emily Madsen: "Listening to My Father Practice" is used with permission of Hill-Stead Museum.

Taylor Mali: "Undivided Attention" from *What Learning Leaves* (Hanover, 2002). Reprinted with the author's permission.

Linda McCarriston: "Birthday Girl: 1950" is reprinted with the author's permission.

Wesley McNair: "The One I Think of Now" from *Fire* by Wesley McNair reprinted by permission of David R. Godine, Publishers, Inc. Copyright © 2002 by Wesley McNair.

Rennie McQuilkin: "Baptism" and "We All Fall Down" are reprinted with the author's permission.

James Merrill: "164 East 72nd Street" from *Collected Poems* by James Merrill, edited by J. D. McClatchy and Stephen Yenser, copyright © 2001 by the Literary Estate of James Merrill at Washington University. Used by permission of Alfred A. Knopf, a division of Random House, Inc.

Honor Moore: "Shenandoah" is reprinted with the author's permission.

Paul Muldoon: "The Mountain Is Holding Out" from *Horse Latitudes* by Paul Muldoon. Copyright © 2006 by Paul Muldoon. Reprinted by permission of Farrar, Straus and Giroux, LLC, and used also by permission of Faber and Faber Limited.

Susanna Myserth: "First Try" is published with the author's permission.

Marilyn Nelson: "Star-Fix" from *Fields of Praise* and "Abba Jacob and Miracles" from *Magnificat* are reprinted with permission of Louisiana University Press. "Aubade (Dawn Song)" is reprinted with permission of the author and Boyds Mill Press.

Pam Nomura: "The Golden Thread" is reprinted with the author's permission.

Hugh Ogden: "Fingers" is used with permission of Hugh Ogden's family.

Sharon Olds: "Mrs. Krikorian" from *The Wellspring* by Sharon Olds, copyright © 1996 by Sharon Olds. Used by permission of Alfred A. Knopf, a division of Random House, Inc, and used also by permission of Random House, UK.

Carolyn Orosz: "Obituary (or the things it should have said)" is used with permission of Hill-Stead Museum.

Grace Paley: "Here" from *Begin Again: Collected Poems* by Grace Paley. Copyright © 2000 by Grace Paley. Reprinted by permission of Farrar, Straus and Giroux, LLC.

Marge Piercy: "The cat's song" from *Mars and Her Children* by Marge Piercy, copyright 1992 by Middlemarsh, Inc. Used by permission of Alfred A. Knopf, a division of Random House, Inc.

Pit Menousek Pinegar: "Shamaal" from *The Possibility of Empty Space* (Andrew Mountain, 1997) is used with the author's permission.

Robert Pinsky: "Poem of Disconnected Parts" from *Gulf Music* by Robert Pinsky. Copyright © 2007 by Robert Pinsky. Reprinted by permission of Farrar, Straus and Giroux, LLC.

Norah Pollard: "Wild Thing" and "Last Light" are reprinted with the author's permission.

Lily Press: "All Natural Drunkard" is used with permission of Hill-Stead Museum.

Bessy Reyna: "Las Dos Camas/Two Beds" first published in *IXOC Amar-Go: Central American Women's Poetry for Peace*, Anglesey, Z., Ed., Granite Press, Maine, 1987. Translated by Susan Sherman and Elinor Randall. Used by permission of Bessy Reyna. "The *Ukiyu-e* Lady in the Snow" first published in *The Battlefield of Your Body* (Hill-Stead Museum, 2005).

Kim Roberts: "My Imaginary Husband" is reprinted with the author's permission.

Kristin Rocha: "Nationalism" is printed with the author's permission.

Kate Rushin: "The Black Back-Ups" and "Going to Canada" are reprinted with the author's permission.

Sonia Sanchez: "Ballad" from *Homegirls and Handgrenades*. Copyright © 1984, 2007 by Sonia Sanchez. Reprinted with permission of The Permissions Company, Inc, on behalf of White Pine Press, www.whitepine.org.

Cheryl Savageau: "First Grade—Standing in the Hall" is printed with the author's permission.

Peter Schmitt: "Packing Plant" appeared in *Renewing the Vows* (David Robert Books, 2007) and is reprinted with the author's permission.

Tim Seibles: "Natasha in a Mellow Mood" from *Hurdy-Gurdy* (Cleveland State University Poetry Series) is reprinted with permission from Cleveland State University Poetry Center.

Vivian Shipley: "Martha Stewart's 10 Commandments for Snow" appears with the author's permission.

Edgar Gabriel Silex: "Distances" is reprinted with the author's permission.

Patricia Smith: "Undertaker" from *Close to Death* (Zoland Books, 1993), "Sweet Daddy" from *Life According to Motown* (Tia Chucha, 1991), and "Why a Colored Girl Will Slice You if You Talk Wrong about Motown" appear by permission of the author.

Gary Soto: "The Skeptics" is used by permission of Gary Soto. Copyright © 1997 by Gary Soto.

Carole Stasiowski: "On Rollerblades" was first published in *Zone 3* (vol. 9, no. 1) and is reprinted with the author's permission.

Jennifer Steele: "To Be the Lighter Shade of Black" is printed with permission of Hill-Stead Museum.

Steve Straight: "At Spike's Garage" is reprinted with the author's permission.

John Surowiecki: "Bolivia Street" was first published by *Burnside Review* and is used with the author's permission.

Zach Sussman: "He Raises His Cup" is printed with permission of Hill-Stead Museum.

Wally Swist: "Guardian Angel" first appeared in *The Larcom Review* and is reprinted with the author's permission.

Tyler Theofilos: "Night Drive" appears with the author's permission.

Elizabeth Thomas: "My Muse" is printed with the author's permission.

Don Thompson: "Where We Live" from *Where We Live* (Parallel Press, 2009). Used with permission of the press and author.

Sue Ellen Thompson: "Remembering My Parents' Sex Life" and "Terms of Endearment" from *The Wedding Boat* (Owl Creek Press, 1995) and *The Leaving: New and Selected Poems* (Autumn House, 2001) are reprinted with the author's permission.

Edwina Trentham: "My Father's Gift" from *Stumbling into the Light* (Antrim House, 2004) is reprinted with the author's permission.

Natasha Trethewey: "His Hands" is included with the author's permission.

Jean Valentine: "Ghost Elephants" first appeared in the *New Yorker* and is reprinted with the author's permission.

David Watts: "winter" is used with the author's permission.

Richard Wilbur: "A Barred Owl" from *Mayflies: New Poems and Translations* by Richard Wilbur. Copyright © 2000 by Richard Wilbur. Reprinted by permission of Houghton Mifflin Harcourt Publishing Company. All rights reserved.

C. K. Williams: "The Coffin Store" from *Wait* by C. K. Williams. Copyright © 2010 by C. K. Williams. Reprinted by permission of Farrar, Straus and Giroux, LLC. Also reprinted by permission of Bloodaxe Books, from *Wait* (2011).

Baron Wormser: "My Last Borders, or Poem Ending with a Homage to W. B. Yeats" from *Scattered Chapters: New & Selected Poems*. Copyright © 2008 by Baron Wormser. Reprinted with the permission of The Permissions Company, Inc., on behalf of Sarabande Books, www.sarabandebooks.org.

Index of Poets

Garnet Books

Food for the Dead: On the Trail of New England's Vampires
by Michael E. Bell

Early Connecticut Silver, 1700–1840
by Peter Bohan and Philip Hammerslough
Introduction and Notes by Erin Eisenbarth

The Connecticut River: A Photographic Journey through the Heart of New England
by Al Braden

Connecticut's Fife & Drum Tradition
by James Clark

Sunken Garden Poetry: 1992–2011
Edited by Brad Davis

The Old Leather Man: Historical Accounts of a Connecticut and New York Legend
by Daniel DeLuca

Post Roads & Iron Horses: Transportation in Connecticut from Colonial Times to the Age of Steam
by Richard DeLuca

Dr. Mel's Connecticut Climate Book
by Dr. Mel Goldstein

Hidden in Plain Sight: A Deep Traveler Explores Connecticut
David K. Leff

Westover School: Giving Girls a Place of Their Own
by Laurie Lisle

Crowbar Governor: The Life and Times of Morgan Gardner Bulkeley
by Kevin Murphy

Fly Fishing in Connecticut: A Guide for Beginners
Kevin Murphy

Water for Hartford: The Story of the Hartford Water Works and the Metropolitan District Commission
by Kevin Murphy

Henry Austin: In Every Variety of Architectural Style
by James F. O'Gorman

Making Freedom: The Extraordinary Life of Venture Smith
by Chandler B. Saint and George Krimsky

Welcome to Wesleyan: Campus Buildings
by Leslie Starr

Gervase Wheeler: A British Architect in America, 1847–1860
by Renée Tribert and James F. O'Gorman

Connecticut in the American Civil War: Slavery, Sacrifice, and Survival
by Matthew Warshauer

Stories in Stone: How Geology Influenced Connecticut History and Culture
by Jelle Zeilinga de Boer